MINNESOTA GARDENS

AN ILLUSTRATED HISTORY

To Loraine,
Happy gardening!
Susan Davis Price

MINNESOTA GARDENS

AN ILLUSTRATED HISTORY

SUSAN DAVIS PRICE

Afton Historical Society Press
Afton, Minnesota

Half title page photo by D.R. Martin.

Frontispiece: Augustus M.P. Cowley residence
at 1994 Summit Avenue in St. Paul about 1918, glass
lantern slide, Minnesota Historical Society.

p. 8 (opposite Contents): Glensheen estate in Duluth,
1930s stereopticon, Glensheen, University of
Minnesota.

Afton Historical Society Press
P.O. Box 100
Afton, MN 55001

PUBLISHER'S NOTE

This book is very close to my heart. The history of Minnesota gardens is a story I have wanted to bring to print for a long time. A couple of years ago I discussed the possibility of such a book with Duncan and Sally MacMillan of Wayzata, Minnesota. They were all for it. Duncan is president of the Afton Historical Society Press; at home he raises prize-winning orchids. Sally was a third-generation gardener whose great love of flowers and trees and shrubs had been passed down to her by her mother and grandmother, both of whom had beautiful gardens in the East. Sally had some of the loveliest gardens in Minnesota, and she was the historian for the Lake Minnetonka Garden Club.

With a little coaxing, Sally agreed to write the Foreword for *Minnesota Gardens*. The two of us had great fun planning this book—over lunch in Wayzata, over lunch in Stillwater, at my house, and at hers. Sally knew a great deal about various Minnesota gardens—who had the best ones, who used to have the best ones, and the professional gardeners behind some of them.

The text for *Minnesota Gardens* was written by Susan Davis Price, who came highly recommended by the Minnesota State Horticultural Society. In the course of her research for this book, Susan collected some really remarkable historic photographs throughout the state. The balance of the photographs are by a number of outstanding Minnesota photographers including D. R. Martin, Lynn Steiner, and Charles J. Johnston. Charles A. Wechsler edited this book. It was designed by the very talented Barbara J. Arney.

In her Foreword, Sally MacMillan talks about admiring her peonies for their fortitude and beauty,

the same qualities that people admired about Sally. Despite being diagnosed with terminal cancer in late 1991, she continued to live a full, productive life. One day when I stopped by to see her, she was down on her hands and knees planting annuals around a small windmill in her front yard. There was something very therapeutic about digging in a garden, smelling the earth, and planting a flower, she said.

Sally's spring garden was at its best, and her beloved peonies in full bloom, when she died in late May 1995. Her memorial cards carried a verse from one of her favorite poems—"The Lord God Planted a Garden" by Dorothy Frances Gurney:

> *The kiss of the sun for pardon,*
> *The song of the birds for mirth—*
> *One is nearer God's heart in a garden*
> *Than anywhere else on earth.*

On August 8, 1995, Wayzata Garden Club members dedicated the Sally MacMillan Memorial Garden at Interfaith Outreach and Community Partners on Grand Avenue in Wayzata.

Minnesota Gardens is also part of Sally MacMillan's legacy. She was looking forward to the publication of this book, and I think she would have been very pleased with it. Because of her, it has special significance for me.

Patricia Condon Johnston
September 1995

CONTENTS

FOREWORD

In Minnesota, better than half of our gardening year is spent hoping and planning.

We imagine how a snow-covered slope will become something gloriously colorful. We draw charts that anticipate resplendent things for a back-yard corner hidden under the brown remains of late autumn. To keep hands busy that are eager for digging and pruning and picking, we page through seed catalogues and garden books.

Once spring arrives, we work feverishly to get our gardens in shape by May and June. During our short growing season, we enjoy a few fleeting months of horticultural delight—from daffodils and tulips through lilies and roses to zinnias and mums—and then it's all over. All too soon.

Even so, brief as our days in the sun may be, I'd happily compare our Minnesota gardens to any throughout the snowbelt.

Recently, for instance, my youngest daughter and I had an opportunity to tour the woodland gardens of a large estate on the East Coast. People told us ahead of time that these particular gardens were fabulous and that we'd love them. Well, the azaleas were out but past their prime, and the rhododendrons hadn't arrived. About all there was to see was the landscaping. Handsome though it was, none of it seemed all that impressive.

Meantime, in Minnesota, everything had turned beautifully green in my absence. I arrived home to find my daffodils had come out and the lilacs in bud. Like many Minnesota gardens, my plantings lack a lot of variety, but they looked prettier to me than most everything I'd seen out East.

We Minnesota gardeners can envy climates that have lush rhododendron and azalea, laurel and magnolia. Who wouldn't like more time in the garden, more time to experiment, more time to delight in their flowers?

But who in Minnesota would *really* give up their lilacs? Their peonies? Their Minnesota wildflowers? I would find it very difficult, because I feel so connected with my gardens and the way they fit into our challenging cycle of seasons.

I'm reminded of the sheer ruggedness of my peonies—how for a quarter of a century they have soldiered through our long, hard winters and thrived here. Like it was yesterday, I remember driving down to a big farm in Faribault and going on a glorious peony binge. I picked out twenty-two varieties, and all but one or two plants have survived. I can't help but admire them for their fortitude and beauty.

After reading *Minnesota Gardens*, I feel much the same about my fellow gardeners in this state—from the pioneers who greeted newcomers with slips of plants to the city planners whose foresight resulted in our beautiful public parks. On the following pages, Susan Price tells us about many individuals—some famous, some obscure—who shared a common bond. Some brought their skills from Europe to create wonderfully designed floral gardens and cemeteries. Some started nurseries and wrote gardening columns. Some were members of the first garden clubs in the state.

Determined to surmount the climate, Minnesota horticulturalists created new varieties of plants and trees that could endure our tough Minnesota winters. Imagine if Horace Greeley—who said he wouldn't live in Minnesota because "you can't grow apples there"—could come back today to feast on our many delicious varieties.

During the first World War, gardens were viewed as an activity to help incorporate newcomers, especially immigrants, into the community as well as to keep young people "off the streets." A few years later, one Depression-era Minnesotan noted that in a garden, "we can get away from the every-day worries and cares."

Minnesota Gardens reminds us what a vital part of this state's history gardening has been. And if you don't know the names of all the human characters, you no doubt will recognize many of the other stars of this story. Pictured on the pages of your favorite seed catalogues, they fill the tables at your local nursery.

It's true that we Minnesotans have been dealt a demanding hand by nature. But I think in a certain way that this is a gift.

We know our gardens' value because we never, *ever* take them for granted—whether they're in full midsummer bloom or only an eager, wintertime glimmer in your mind's eye.

Sarah Stevens (Sally) MacMillan
Historian
Lake Minnetonka Garden Club

Sally MacMillan chose this intimate view of her patio garden in the summer of 1994 to accompany her Foreword.

D.R. Martin

11

PREFACE

Shortly after starting this book, I told a friend about the project, a history of Minnesota gardens. His response was quick: "That'll be a short book." The assessment was off the mark, of course, but memorable. How could anyone be so sure there would be nothing to write about? My friend wasn't a gardener, which is a partial explanation. But the important reasons are less obvious.

As my research proceeded, I began to appreciate his reaction and to conclude that the story of gardening is indeed a "secret" history. Without the sustaining human touch, even the loveliest gardens languish. Most of the wonderful landscapes I discovered have long disappeared. Unlike architecture, which can survive for a time if left untended, gardens go to "wrack and ruin" within a season or two. Weeds move in; shrubs take over; pools crack. Soon, even award-winning gardens like Father Pomije's garden at Olivia are completely forgotten.

Moreover, gardening is usually ignored in standard histories. Look in vain for a description of a settler's garden in studies of pioneer life. Search for the importance of plants to the Victorian in works about nineteenth-century customs. It would be easy to conclude that gardens were simply "fluff," not important enough to be covered.

Not so. A look at firsthand documentation reveals a wealth of information showing that the "leading lights" of horticulture were leaders of the community. R.J. Mendenhall, for example, member of the Minnesota State Horticultural Society and Minneapolis's first florist, was also a president of State National Bank of Minneapolis, town treasurer, and secretary of the Board of Education. Joseph Underwood was mayor of Lake City, owner of Jewell Nurseries and active in the Minnesota Horticultural Society.

In addition, the community viewed the garden and gardening as essential. Most nineteenth- and early twentieth-century county histories, for example, devote a chapter to horticulture, describing greenhouses and horticulture societies. At biennial meetings of the Minnesota State Horticultural Society, members attested to the importance of gardening in their lives. City boosters pointed with pride to parks and gardens. Clearly, gardens were an integral part of community life.

What sort of garden was I looking for? After all, gardens come in many configurations. The vegetable plot was certainly necessary to Minnesota's history, but in this study "pleasure-grounds" were my focus. According to the Victorian, such spots were "laid out or ornamented for purposes of pleasure or amusement or naturally adapted to such use." By this definition, parks and even cemeteries were as important as private gardens.

The "pleasure-ground," not the vegetable plot, elicited intense commentary and strong emotions from earlier Minnesota gardeners. Food crops are vital, but they are more likely to call forth technical essays. John Harris, the orchardist, could discuss the proper treatment of apples with ease and competence, but on floriculture he waxed poetic. Flower gardens, he wrote, "point us back to a 'Paradise Lost' and urge us a Paradise to regain. . . . [They] engage the intellect, and open fields of inexhaustible treasure which the longest life is far too short to fully explore." Late twentieth-century Minnesotans may not express themselves with such flourish, yet they can understand Harris's sentiments. What gardener doesn't feel a bit of paradise within his garden?

Where, then, does the researcher go for the garden's role in community life? My first clues came from the diaries and correspondence of early Minnesota men and women. In letters home or careful daily records, they testify to the essential nature of gardening activities. Sophie Bost of Chanhassen, for example, wrote about her garden "which has not turned out as well as it should have . . . because of the drought" and asks her mother-in-law to send more seeds from Europe, because "I love to care for my flowers, especially those that come from our old home."

Journals and newspapers offered a wealth of information.

Lyman Ford's *The Minnesota Farmer and Gardener*, which ran for two years in the 1860s, gave a full picture of horticulture and agriculture in the young state, listing plants that could or did grow here, and describing exemplary and deficient landscapes wherever he encountered them.

Vintage seed and nursery catalogues, available at the Minnesota Historical Society and the Andersen Horticultural Library at the Minnesota Landscape Arboretum, provided an accurate record of plants sold locally and trends in garden styles.

Collections can be wonderful, and Minnesota has many fine ones. But without staff to help negotiate their sometimes byzantine arrangements, the best library or historical society will remain only partially available to the user.

Fortunately, many people came to my rescue along the way.

Archivists at county historical societies throughout the state were resourceful and eager to respond to my unusual requests. No one seems to have asked for garden history before. No matter, they all found photos, garden club information, and stories about historic sites.

Richard Isaacson at the Andersen Library gave me a detailed look at library holdings, supplying information about garden history at the same time, and made photocopying a painless procedure. Dorothy Johnson at the Minnesota Horticultural Society opened their slide collection, complete run of the *Minnesota Horticulturist*, and historical files, providing easy access to much essential information.

The Minnesota Historical Society became my "second home" for more than a year. All the staff—librarians, stack attendants, and photocopiers—took a personal interest in the project and continually were on the lookout for items that might fit with my research. Dallas Lindgren explained the intricacies of manuscripts, especially the arcane arrangements of railroad records. Tony Greiner and Lori Leirdahl were on hand every Saturday to point out sources I might have missed, to help select the "best" photos for the book, and to share in the small joys and frustrations of research.

To them and all the others unnamed, I send my thanks.

Peter Olin, Roberta Sladky, Mary Maguire Lerman, Dan McClelland, Lynn Steiner, Michele Lee Amundsen, Paul Maravelas, Michael Lane, Yvonne Bublitz, Dr. Bardwell Smith, and others took time to read and comment on errors in the manuscript. Their work has made the final product more accurate than it would have been.

Friend and confidante C. B. Rykken read and proofed most of the chapters, helping me to say more clearly and forcefully what I had meant to say. For his nearly year-long effort I am thankful. In the last desperate weeks Jessica Blue jumped in to help with photos, errands, and a massive bibliography. Publisher Pat Johnston and editor Chuck Wechsler at the Afton Historical Society Press were always encouraging and upbeat.

A special thanks is due Minnesota landscape architect Herb Baldwin. Not only did he give wise counsel about gardens, but late in the project, he accepted my invitation to write the epilogue.

My husband Mike and our sons Peter and Dan may have felt neglected these last twelve months. If so, they never expressed the feeling; instead, they seemed excited about my efforts and encouraged me when the going was slow.

Especially I want to thank my father who always read, saved, and commented on everything I've written. It is his love of gardens and his belief in me that has made this possible.

This book, then, is dedicated to my father who communicated to me his passion for gardening, to my husband who indulges my interest, and to my sons who have inherited it.

S. D. P.

Sally Beyer/Greg Ryan

INTRODUCTION

A gentleman from Pennsylvania rode over the Minnesota prairies during July of 1857. In a series of letters home, he described what he saw.

No one who has not visited this region can form any adequate idea of

the grandeur and magnificence and beauty of these Nature's meadows.

They spread out in their illimitable expanse like the ocean, filling the

mind with awe and wonder. The flowers run wildly on these prairies.

In fact they are nature's flower gardens—planted by the same hand

that planted the stars in the canopy above.[1]

The author, known only by the pseudonym "Viator," published his remarks in the *Venango Spectator*, the newspaper of Franklin, Pennsylvania. His observations would echo through the decades, as tourists and homesteaders poured into the virgin country. Many were struck by the clean beauty of Minnesota's fields and woods. In diaries and correspondence, they wrote about the flowers, the trees, the terrain. And like the visitor from Pennsylvania, they saw the land not merely as a lovely slice of nature, but as a "garden," to be savored surely, but also to be harvested if need arose.

Not all responses were positive, however. Women, in particular, were often overwhelmed by the prairie's vast, treeless expanse. But as they cultivated the land and made one corner of it their own, most women found ways to appreciate the virgin landscape, the blue sky, and the clean air. Especially they noticed the flowers, commenting on their abundance, observing their colors, enjoying their fragrance. They gathered bouquets and decorated their homes. Often they shared the blossoms with friends. In appreciating the wildflowers, they remembered the gardens they had left behind, and anticipated the gardens they would create in their adopted land.

SETTLERS

&

EARLY

STATEHOOD

1840 - 1870

*Despite adverse circumstances, these
Morrison County settlers have planted roses
and trees to help beautify their log home.*

HOMESTEADING

If you have some flower seeds that can be sent in a letter, think of me,

dear Mother and I'll be very grateful to you for them. I love so much to

care for my flowers, especially those that come from our old home.

Sophie Bost, in a letter to her mother-in-law in Switzerland, 1862.[2]

In 1849 Minnesota was recognized as a territory by the United States Congress, opening a floodgate of immigration which continued unabated through the century. Thanks to the press and to the natural advantages available here, thousands of people from Europe and the East Coast began to pour into the state, claiming land in towns and countryside.

Initially, finding shelter occupied the families' energies. In haste, they constructed homes: log cabins in wooded areas, dugouts on the prairie, and frame structures in town. Once the building was accomplished, the family, usually the mother and children, planted the garden.

Most of these early gardens—urban or rural— were fairly utilitarian. The real urgency, especially in the country, was for securing enough food to carry the family through the harsh winter. Potatoes, beans, and corn were planted in the roughly cleared earth, often between tree stumps.

Close behind the need for food was the need for simple remedies to cure common ailments. Isolated as the settlers were, with doctors rarely seen, responsibility for the family's health fell to the women. Old "receipt" books and traditional cures passed down through the family gave them a store of remedies to use. Chief among these medicines was the use of herbs. Plants thought to promote the healing of bones, to reduce fevers, to "settle the stomach," or to help ease a "cold in the lungs" played an important part in the lives of many pioneers.[3]

What they needed then was what is today called a "kitchen" garden—informal beds close by the house where everything could be grown together. In dooryard gardens, often set off from the surrounding countryside by a split-rail fence, women planted plots of tansy and catnip beside clumps of iris, with potatoes and gooseberries a little farther off. Among the herbs could be found boneset, said to make the patient sweat, or wormwood and chamomile for tonics of various kinds.[4] Feverfew, the pioneer's aspirin, was considered good for a toothache.[5] Tansy and costmary (called Bible Leaf by settlers) were grown to repel insects. As late as the 1890s, Farmer Seed Company of Faribault advertised "Aromatic, Sweet, Pot and Medicinal Herbs" in its mail-order catalogue, among them horehound seeds for coughs, rue for croup, hyssop for asthma and chest colds, and thyme for headaches.[6]

To supplement what she herself could grow, the homesteader looked to the woods and fields for healing plants. Native Americans were one source of information;[7] neighbors were another. Orcella Rexford described her grandmother's use of native plants in her book, *101 Weeds and Wildlings*.

When Grandmother was a settler in Minnesota, she found her knowledge of herbs came in handy to help the other settlers when they were sick and there were no doctors to be had. . . . [Among the plants she looked for were] the delicate green spires of sweet Blue Flag to be followed with ethereal lavendar blossoms, beloved as a nerve remedy [or] the magenta blossoms of Wild Geranium, used as an astringent. . . . The Stinging Nettle was regarded with high favor . . . boiled like spinach, they were used as a "blood purifier" and an "iron tonic."[8]

Clearly, much of the pioneer's time was taken up in the essentials of caring for the family; preparing food and clothing were large tasks in themselves. Health care and cleaning chores demanded more. Circumstances were not auspicious for making ornamental gardens. Yet in spite of numerous constraints, women worked to convert their cabins into cozy homes for their families. Adding flowers and shrubs was a ready way to create a pleasant, intimate space that set the house apart from the wildness around it.[9]

Emily Polasek, remembering her early homesteading years in northern Minnesota, wrote: "Mother planted hollyhocks, larkspur and Oriental poppies around the house, had a big flower garden by the barn, and even planted flowers around the outhouse. Our house, nestled among the big trees, looked like a picture in a storybook."[10]

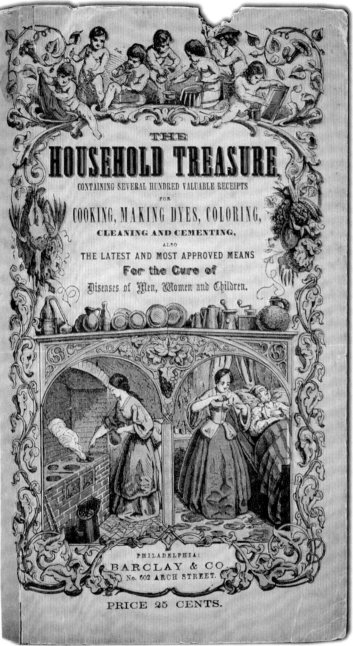

Minnesota Historical Society

Receipt books were standard guides for mid-nineteenth century families. This one from 1864 contained recipes for cooking, making dyes and clothing, as well as for preparing medicines.

Remnants of these early plantings can be seen around many surviving pioneer homesteads, where the lilacs and daylilies have outlasted the houses. Near Moorhead, German immigrant Randolph Probstfield planted thirteen peony plants, one for each member of his family. By the late twentieth century, the farm was abandoned, but the peonies continued to flourish, evidence of the care once lavished there.[11]

What the settlers planted was dependent on ideas they brought from former gardens and on the availability of seeds and shrubs. Annuals that grew easily from seed were popular. Besides petunias and alyssum, pioneers planted portulacas, verbenas, sweet williams, and larkspur. Sunflowers were favorites on the prairie; in fact, some women grew them atop their dugouts.[12] Geraniums bloomed in tubs by the door or gate. Perennials such as iris and daylilies, which divide easily, were common. Peonies and old-fashioned roses, especially Harison's Yellow, flourished almost everywhere. Flowering shrubs were the sturdy standards—lilacs, mock orange, spirea, and hydrangea, which the settlers often called snowball.

· — ◆ — ·

Jane Grey Swisshelm was a reporter from the East Coast and the sister of St. Cloud resident Elizabeth Mitchell. An ardent abolitionist and suffragist, Swisshelm lived and wrote in St. Cloud from 1857 to 1863.

Trillium was noted by early settlers as one of Minnesota's woodland beauties.

Considering the relative isolation of many homesteads, how did the pioneers obtain seeds and plants? Many seem to have thought of their gardens before setting off to the new land. They tucked seeds inside trunks and tore vines off front porches as they left. Some were like Philena Pickett. In moving west toward Albert Lea in 1860, she packed her precious rose bush in the wagon along with the clothes and provisions.[13]

Others requested seeds and "slips" from relatives and friends. Seeds fit easily into letters from home; shrubs shared space with more practical items aboard steamers and later on trains. In 1859 Jane Grey Swisshelm, sojourning in St. Cloud, acknowledged the gift of lilacs and Blush and Damask roses sent to her on the steamer *Enterprise* by friends in St. Anthony.[14]

Settlers were happy to share their surplus; many plants, like lilies of the valley, multiply quickly. When women got together

· — ◆ — ·

Old roses, lush and fragrant, were frequently brought with the settlers and planted as the house was built.

Settlers favored reliable perennials like the bleeding heart, now grown at Gammelgarden, the Swedish heritage museum in Scandia.

with others in their community, a favorite gift was seeds or "starts" of plants. Some transplanted flowers and blooming shrubs from fields and woods. Norwegian immigrant Gjertrud Hilleboe, for example, who first feared the new country, came to love the "beautiful trees, shrubs, vines, berries, grasses and wild flowers. Many of these she transplanted to beautify her house and garden."[15]

Plants were available commercially as well. After the Civil War, itinerant salesmen moved through the territories, selling trees and shrubs. These "tree peddlers," as they were sometimes called, carried books with lusciously colored plates, sure to tempt the isolated farm wife.[16] Others, once rail travel was widespread, set up shop in train stations, knowing that newly arrived settlers would be a ready market. Some of these men sold plants of questionable quality or plants not hardy enough for Minnesota's climate. Newspaper and agricultural journalists of the time penned acid words warning against the worst of these, calling them "borers, barklice . . . and foreign tree hucksters."[17]

Mail-order companies did a box-office business. At first the major suppliers were from the East—Vick's, Burpee's, and Ferry. But local nurseries and seed companies began turning up in the late 1850s and increased in number along with the population. Groveland Nursery, located at St. Anthony between St. Paul and Minneapolis, issued its first catalogue in 1855. Farmer Seed Company opened in 1858 in Faribault.

In 1862 Sophie Bost of Chanhassen wrote of ordering two lilacs, serenga, and a number of other plants and flowers from a nursery in Wisconsin. She hoped the plants would be a success. "The nursery is in the same latitude and climate as we are and ships a great number of trees to Minnesota."[18]

Still, most of the early settlers viewed the prairie and woodlands as extensions of the gardens within their gates. Field flowers and wild fruit were certainly more abundant and varied than plants cultivated by the family. Early nurseryman Lyman Ford lamented that "farmers depend too much on the wild fruits" instead of devoting sufficient acreage to cultivation.[19] But Tilla Deen, in *Chronicles of a Minnesota Pioneer*, remembered the "wild things" of her childhood in more pleasant terms.

There were many wild flowers. Our favorites were the wild crocus

that covered a small hill near home. As soon as the snow was gone in

the spring, Caroline and I would load the younger sisters in a cart

Father had made for us, and take daily trips to this hill to see if the

flowers were blooming. While they lasted we brought home arms full

of them every day. Around the lake were choke cherry and plum trees.

When they were in bloom we always had the house full of blossoms.[20]

Not all pioneer efforts were successful, of course. The climate was too harsh, the rains too unpredictable to guarantee results. Even Sophie Bost mentioned seeds from Switzerland that failed to germinate and plants that did poorly. In 1877 Hortense Share of Rosemount described her experiences for the Minnesota State Horticultural Society.

The first two summers were exceptionally dry and the winds on the

prairie simply abominable. The choice shrubbery, roses and vines

we brought with us died. The flower seeds I planted in June came

up beautifully, in September after the rain. The bulbs, several kinds

and choice, perished the first winter.[21]

Conditions such as these were reason enough for some settlers to decide the effort was too great. Not Hortense Share, who wrote, "With me flowers are a necessity. . . . I turned to the wild flowers, for flowers I must have. The many beautiful kinds on the prairie, in the brush and on the shore were a source of continual delight."[22]

For some settlers, growing a garden was sufficient in itself. However, flowers are mentioned frequently enough in accounts of the period to indicate they played a larger role in pioneers' lives. Many recalled bouquets on the table and dried flowers over the doors inside. Flowers and other plants marked special events— weddings, funerals, family gatherings. Weddings near Melrose, a predominantly German settlement, called for the "hanging of the wreath."[23] On the Sunday before the wedding, young men made a wreath and a heavy rope of green branches and vines interwoven with flowers. The rope was draped over the door of the bride's house, the wreath, carried in procession around the house as the young people sang German love songs.

Beginning in the mid-1850s, county and territorial fairs claimed a prominent place in the pioneers' social life. From the earliest occasions, women entered flowers and potted plants while their husbands offered corn and wheat.[24] Fairs in Minneapolis and St. Paul attracted entries from neighboring counties. A lengthy account of St. Paul's 1860 fair appeared in *The Minnesotan.*

On approaching the place, the cool evergreen bower that spanned,

arch-like, the side-walk, indicated the spot. We entered. An odor of

flowers—ten thousand flowers—saluted us. . . .We now come to the

finest vegetable display of the Fair—that of Martin D. Clarke of

McLean township. He had the best pair of cucumbers, and the best

basketful. . . . Amidst Mr. Clarke's creditable display, was a large

dish of wild flowers, embracing flowers of water and land—the white

water lily, the yellow, and more modest flowers of prairie and hillside.

. . . A bouquet of Wild Flowers, gathered on the Prairie

at Hamilton, in Scott county, by Mrs.Ella Hanks,

elicited many expressions of admiration. . . . Nor did

a display of Poppies, from the Episcopal Mission, pass

without notice. The crowd who attended were delighted.[25]

Most of the early ornamental gardens were fairly basic—a few flowers planted by the front door, a vine along the fence. But some settlers, such as Henry Swartwoudt, who lived on a farm midway between Prairieville and Cannon City, had grounds that were "handsomely laid out in lawn and flower garden, ornamental and fruit trees."[26] Others, like the energetic Sophie Bost, seem to have had extensive gardens from the beginning. In September 1859, a year after she arrived in America, Sophie wrote home: "My flower garden is still very pretty, witness a beautiful bouquet that occupies the center of the table I am writing on. . . . But wait until next year when I'll have a garden that will amaze everybody—flowers, and heaps of vegetables."[27]

FENCES & FLOWERS

It was interesting to observe with what fond care plants and shrubs were brought from the old homes to adorn the new. It was not rare to see roses, peonies, lilies, snow-balls, and other shrubs planted out in the sod even before the house went up.

Emily Atwater, *Pioneer Life in Minneapolis, from a Woman's Standpoint*, 1894.[28]

Minnesota's population exploded during the boom years shortly after mid-century. The census showed 6,000 people in 1850 and 172,000 just ten years later. New towns were platted at an amazing rate—seven hundred between 1855 and 1857! Each town believed it might become a major metropolis. Clearly, Minnesota was a state on the move as citizens felt the excitement of building new communities westward to the Dakotas.

Despite the euphoria, the day-to-day reality of town life was often one of inconvenience and hardship. Food supplies, especially in towns far away from the Twin Cities, arrived erratically. Many settlers maintained vegetable gardens rather than trust to the mercy of shippers. Most streets were simply rutted wagon roads; sidewalks, when they existed, were made of boards. Transportation was not always reliable. Conditions were hardly encouraging for planting gardens or for beautifying the town.

And yet in the midst of the dust and mud, Minnesotans approached horticultural challenges with characteristic pioneer pluck. Residents in small towns built fences and planted flowers. In 1869 thirteen women met in Austin to form the "Ladies Floral Club," a group to encourage the study of floriculture, beautify the town, and establish a circulating library. Two gentlemen in St. Paul in 1860 published the first Minnesota agriculture/horticulture journal. In 1866 twelve plantsmen formed the Minnesota Fruit Growers Society, which two years later became the Minnesota Horticultural Society. These were remarkable individuals, to be sure, fueled by the optimism of the times. Still, their pioneer efforts were aided by the fact that they lived in communities where ideas could be shared and tasks divided up. Their accomplishments laid the groundwork for the thriving gardening community that followed.

As new towns sprouted, so did gardens. The first town yards were similar to their rural counterparts: vegetables, fruit trees, and flowers in close proximity, with fences an essential feature of the gardenscape. Besides being decorative, they protected vegetables and flowers from stray hogs and cattle.

25

Depending on the homeowner's affluence, fences were made of wrought iron, wood, or split rails.

Jane Grey Swisshelm reported great disparity in Minnesota towns. St. Cloud was a fine example—"spring fences going up around every . . . house, and smiling gardens peeped out at one." Another village left much to be desired—"not a fence worth the name, no trees, no shrubbery, no garden—I did not see one man, woman, or child doing anything to make their home look like places to live in."[29]

Once they were more settled, gardeners began to cultivate lawns. A smooth lawn was not yet the status symbol it would become by the century's end, but good grass was worth some effort. In May 1860, the editor of the *New Era* newspaper in Sauk Rapids reported on his successful experiment to grow Kentucky blue grass around his house.[30]

Townspeople, having cut so many trees to make way for construction, began replacing them to obtain shade. In the role of hectoring uncles, newspapers urged citizens to plant. In 1856 the

St. Paul *Pioneer* recommended elm. Others suggested ash, maple, and box elder.[31] Photographs of the time commonly show a young, rough sapling next to a newly built house. As early as 1858 fur trader, mill owner, and community leader Richard Chute transplanted three thousand cottonwood trees along the streets of St. Anthony.

Ornamental plants seem to have been a valuable commodity, if their theft is any indication. One report from St. Paul stated:

Many . . . are complaining bitterly of . . . some scamps who go about stealing their choicest shrubs and flowers. Some time ago Mr. Farrington spoke . . . about his beautiful Perpetual Roses . . . brought all the way from Rochester, and after having them in the yard a few days they suddenly disappeared. . . . And now . . . Mr. Nicols . . . informs us that somebody has infested his grounds and has stolen some of Mrs. Nicols' favorite plants.[32]

Even during this early period, there were people of means. These citizens had the leisure and wealth to plan and maintain gardens of great beauty and elaborate design. From time to time the local press would report on one of these gardens: fine homes and fine gardens were considered newsworthy. In 1859 the St. Paul *Daily Pioneer and Democrat* wrote at length about the home of Dr. Alfred Elisha Ames, Minneapolis civic leader and one of the city's first physicians.

Dr. A. E. Ames . . . enjoys the reputation of possessing one of the finest and most expensive flower gardens in the Northwest. Boquets [sic] culled from his parterres and arranged by the fine taste of the German man who superintends the garden, are eagerly sought for at home and abroad. Some sent to Chicago last summer were much admired for their superior fragrance and vividness of color. The Dr. spares no pains and expense in improving and adorning his grounds,

and making them one of the most attractive places of resort in the vicinity. . . . Those of our readers who can make it convenient to pay a visit to the garden of Dr. Ames, will be amply rewarded by an hour's stroll among the flowers. The collection of plants and shrubs is very choice, and the arrangement about the grounds is upon a scale of liberality and taste.[33]

One of the era's most interesting individuals was Lyman Ford, proprietor of Groveland Nursery and originator of *The Minnesota Farmer and Gardener*, the state's first agriculture/horticulture magazine. Ford was from New York state. In 1850 he "caught the western fever,"[34] as he later explained it, and came to Minnesota. After two years of teaching French and organizing a singing school,

·—◆—·

Flower-loving Dr. Alfred Elisha Ames, photographed about 1869, built the first greenhouse in St. Anthony. He hired a young German florist, William Buchendorf, to tend his garden. Later, Buchendorf started his own greenhouse and gardening business.

Ford started his fledgling nursery by transplanting some apple trees that grew in his dooryard. The nursery was located on Raymond Avenue three blocks south of what is now University Avenue. By 1855 he had printed a catalogue offering "fruit and ornamental trees, shrubs, roses, and dahlias."

In the catalogue, Ford included thirty-one different ornamental shrubs, among them flowering almond and five kinds of lilacs. For fifty cents apiece, gardeners could buy evergreens or twenty-one varieties of deciduous trees—locust and larch along with ash and elm. Gooseberries, asparagus, and other small fruits and vegetables were available.

His rose selection included over one hundred named varieties, enough to tempt the most ardent rose fancier. Besides noisettes and climbers he offered robust hybrid perpetuals—La Reine and Baron Prevost—and exquisite tea roses—Belle Amalie and Bonjour among them. Ford wisely recommended that "most kinds of roses should be somewhat protected during winter, by covering with leaves or litter."[35] The catalogue sold a complete line of flower seeds, and many annuals and perennials. As a further incentive, Ford offered easy delivery.

Stages are passing several times during the day, near our

Establishment, so that we are enabled to send small packages to

persons ordering in either town, at almost any hour.[36]

In 1855 Ford married Abbie Guild, herself a dedicated gardener. Before leaving Sandusky, Ohio, where they were wed,

Minnesota State Horticultural Society

Minnesota Historical Society

— ◆ —

Abbie dug roots of two kinds of plants—May pinks ("fragrant favorites our mothers so dearly loved," said Lyman)[37] and another flower whose name Ford could not later recall. These plants thrived under Abbie's care and were soon spread to many other flower lovers in Minnesota.

Ford considered his wife a partner in the nursery. There were always certain plants in the greenhouse called "Mrs. Ford's plants," which she exhibited at fairs and gave as presents to friends. Her arrangements were prize-winning and novel. For one of the first commencements at the University of Minnesota, Abbie prepared an arrangement that "created more of a surprise than anything seen, owing to the large red bloom of *Phyllocactus Ackermanie* [the cactus orchid]."[38]

In 1869 Abbie introduced the tuberose at the St. Paul wedding of merchant E. D. K. Randall and Sarah Cavender, daughter of early settler Abram Cavender. Sarah's was the first bridal bouquet ever seen in Minnesota containing such flowers, and soon other brides began requesting them.

For almost thirty years the Ford nursery was a thriving enterprise, offering plants not previously available in Minnesota. According to one observer, the nursery was "a fairy-like spot" exhibiting "refined and cultivated taste in the arrangement of grounds and the innumerable variety of flowers and plants." [39]

Groveland Nursery was not Lyman Ford's only contribution to the local gardening scene, however. *The Minnesota Farmer and*

Gardener, his valuable though short-lived journal, remains a rich chronicle of the state's agricultural and horticultural history.

The first issue appeared November 1860, and the periodical thereafter came out monthly, full of information for farmers, gardeners, politicians, businessmen, naturalists, teachers, and "owners of a lot or yard." There was much to help the "ladies," as well, who would learn "many things that will be of use to them either in the family or flower garden."[40] Ford promised a journal "suitable for their parlors and drawing rooms."[41] In every issue he cajoled and prodded his readers to improve their yards and farms.

During November and December [he advised in December 1860] there is a great dearth of flowers. Everyone, therefore, should have the Chrysanthemum. . . . At this season a few good specimens . . . are especially appropriate and very showey. . . . Besides the Chrysanthemum is so easily cultivated, that any family may have it.[42]

Several months later he urged, "Every house, either in town or country, should have a few evergreens about it, if there is room to admit trees of any kind."[43]

Frequently, he held up examples of local gardeners who were doing well or mentioned others who could work harder. In May 1861, for instance, he wrote of "Dr. Ames [who] has added more to his list of evergreens and shrubs with his large stock of bedding plants and roses. . . . The citizens of St. Anthony must look to their laurels, or rather we should say Evergreens, roses, dahlias, etc."[44]

In addition, each issue was filled with solid horticultural advice, including a regular column, "Work for the Month," giving subscribers lists of chores to be handled that season. Despite his best efforts to win subscribers—offering premiums of shrubs and trees and "papers of choice flower seeds"—Ford failed to garner adequate

support to keep the journal afloat.[45] The April 1862 issue was his last, ending the publication that territorial legislator William H. Nobles described as "suitable to the real wants and interests of the citizens."[46] A few years later Ford resumed giving horticultural advice through a column in the St. Paul paper, the *Daily Press*.

Health problems compelled the Fords to sell the greenhouse and grounds in 1883 and "try the climate of California."[47] In San Diego, Ford recovered his strength and started a nursery, growing cactus, begonias, ferns, and raising seeds for eastern nurserymen. Although they never returned to Minnesota, the Fords maintained a deep affection for their cherished state and its horticulture.

It takes imagination to strive for beauty in the midst of rough, unsympathetic conditions, but the trait seems to have been widespread among the state's early settlers. One group of women in Austin looked out over their raw, muddy town and envisioned "well kept lawns, flower gardens and a library."[48]

In 1869, when Austin was in need of all the usual civic improvements—schools, a courthouse, public buildings, roads—thirteen women organized the Ladies Floral Club for "their mutual benefit and to beautify the village."[49]

The idea was first proposed by Esther Morse, the minister's wife, "a great lover of flowers herself and also desirous of seeing others enjoy Nature's beauties."[50] Their husbands, however, were "not so keen about the idea, [because] they wanted no 'blue stocking' wives, seeking publicity and planning foolish village expenditures which would have to be financed by the men."[51]

Still, Mrs. Morse and the others were not to be dissuaded. These were educated women who "longed for the attractive surroundings of their former houses in the east."[52] One had been a French teacher and was admitted to the bar. Another had a B.A. and M.A. from

•——◆——•

Mower County Historical Society

Esther Morse organized Minnesota's first women's club, the Ladies Floral Club in Austin.

Alfred University in New York. Several had studied at music conservatories in Boston and Cincinnati. They had the interest and ability to proceed with their plans. Accordingly, on March 16, 1869, the women met at the home of Mrs. Allen to draw up a constitution. Unknowingly, they were organizing the first women's club in Minnesota, the fifth in the United States. At monthly meetings (there were fifty members several months later), they shared knowledge of plants and gardens.[53] The effect was immediate, as the minutes show.

No little yard so tiny and humble but found space for a little patch

of floral beauties. Every window was filled with pots of various

sizes and shapes . . . pinks and roses of humble origin

found they could thrive in mother earth placed in

broken cups and rusty basins, if tended with

care and loving hands.[54]

So successful was the enterprise that the women organized a floral show of their gardens, exhibiting their "beauty and fragrance before the public."[55] Proceeds would be used to establish a circulating library in Austin.

On the appointed day, the women furnished the room with "flowers in garlands, flowers in baskets, flowers in pots on stands, till the beholder was fairly dazzled with beauty."[56] The two evenings' entertainment—essays and poems about flowers the first night and music the second—netted over $100. Continuing with the shows and their library plans, by 1884 the women had amassed a collection of 2,300 volumes and procured a room in the new courthouse where they served as volunteer librarians.[57]

Twenty years later the club helped bring a Carnegie Library to town, turning over its 3,500 books to the new library. Throughout the century members continued to aid other civic enterprises, particularly child welfare and public health. In 1968 the Floral Club celebrated its centennial.[58] The group continues to thrive, justly proud of over one hundred years of service.

Anyone who will journey two days by steamer, rail, and ferry, toting twenty kinds of apples and a variety of other fruit, is someone to be reckoned with. So it was with John Harris, a little-known grower in La Crescent who traveled to St. Paul and the Minnesota State Fair in 1866. Harris had spent ten years developing an apple that could withstand Minnesota winters. His exhibit that year was so outstanding that area plantsmen were inspired to meet and organize the State Fruit Growers Association, which eventually became the Minnesota Horticultural Society.[59]

Raising fruit trees had proved to be a chancy venture for early Minnesotans; many varieties they tried winter-killed or produced poor-quality fruit. In fact, Horace Greeley had said publicly, "I would not live in Minnesota because you can't grow apples there."[60] His remark gave fruit growers even more impetus to produce a tasty, reliable product. When John Harris showed up at the fair with a large quantity of fine apples, the plantsmen rallied.

On a rainy October 3, 1866, a dozen or so men met beneath the State Fair grandstand. They pledged to meet regularly, to promote fruit-growing, and to find varieties that would succeed here.[61] That small band grew; by 1868 there were forty-two members who expanded their mission to embrace all aspects of horticulture. Through the years they gave away thousands of seeds and published lists of proven varieties of shrubs, flowers, and trees. They encouraged the University of Minnesota to establish an experimental station and published the *Minnesota Horticulturist,* the longest-running journal of its kind in the state. Now called the Minnesota State Horticultural Society, the organization has over sixteen thousand members and continues to be a force in state horticulture activities.

•—◆—•

Successfully establishing the apple orchard business was an important step in Minnesota horticulture. These pickers worked at Sunnyside Orchards at La Crescent, owned by John Harris (inset).

D.R. Martin

VICTORIAN

GARDENS

1870 - 1910

—◆—

Spring bulb display in the Sunken Garden,
Como Conservatory, 1995.

PLACES OF DELIGHT

Floriculture shuts out the darkness of sin and lifts the veil to refreshing bowers,

luxurious verdure, pure crystal streams and breezes. The cultivation of flowers,

whether it be the tiny plant in the cracked cup of the poor man's cottage or the

stately palm . . . in palatial gardens and crystal palaces, is wielding an influence

to elevate the human race which no one . . . can tell, no pen describe.

John S. Harris, La Crescent, read at a meeting of the Minnesota State Horticultural Society, July 4, 1872.[62]

Horticultural remnants from the early days of Minnesota are few—peonies by an abandoned farmstead, a line of box elders on the prairie, and, of course, the Minnesota State Horticultural Society. But artifacts from the later decades of the nineteenth century are abundant. The Gates Ajar in St. Paul's Como Park (pictured in an early photo, right), the Schell Brewery gardens in New Ulm, Lakewood Cemetery in Minneapolis, to name a few, all date to the late 1800s.

After the Civil War, widening affluence and stability, in conjunction with a sweeping national interest in things horticultural, laid the foundation for a thriving gardening community. Increasing numbers of Minnesotans found themselves with more money and more time to spend it. Certainly, there were ready supplies of seeds and plant material and sufficient information about gardening.

Technological advances in transportation and communications made life more convenient. The railroad and postal service connected the entire state with the East Coast, speeding plants and seeds across the countryside. Local nurseries and seedsmen and women carried the old standbys in addition to new varieties.

Gardening journals such as *The Horticulturist* and *Ladies Floral Cabinet*, both produced in New York, found their way into many Minnesota homes. Improvements in heating systems and glass production fostered the development of greenhouses and hotbeds. County horticultural societies encouraged gardening and spread information about plant-growing; their annual fairs, offering premiums for the best specimens, were exciting events.[63]

Although ready supplies of plants and helpful advice certainly fostered an interest in gardening, these factors alone cannot fully explain the great surge of horticultural activity. Indeed, gardening filled a multitude of needs: it offered the great advantage of being both familiar and exotic, soothing as well as fascinating.

The image of the garden was a familiar one to nineteenth-century Minnesotans. Immigrants arriving during the 1870s and 1880s, many of them from Germany and Scandinavia, were products of agrarian societies. They brought with them a

knowledge and love of gardening, and they were determined to make the wilderness "blossom like a rose." To create a place of delight was to lay claim to the land, doubly important to people formerly denied the chance to own arable property.

One settler, a man called Henchen from Germany's Rhine Valley, made his garden near the Bloomington ferry in 1870. A neighbor, Minnie Tapping, saw Henchen as a man who "taught [her] of the sky, the trees, the flowers and bees."

There was no public road leading to his spot but he established himself by using the clay river bank, from which he made bricks for a comfortable house. He . . . built his own beehives and . . . rows and rows of symmetrical trellises up the hillsides.

Back of his house . . . was the apple of my eye, his flower garden. My great love of flowers dates back to the delphiniums and gorgeous tulips of that day. I can smell in memory the sweetness of the new roses that he propagated from the old blush rose bush, the rare violet from his common Johnny-jumpup. I can see him snipping off his grape cuttings, tying them with willow strings, to cross with his beautiful Delawares and Rogers.[64]

Often, recreating the gardens of their past provided a link to the lands the immigrants had left behind. When New Ulm brewer August Schell built his ten-room home and laid out the garden, he paid homage to the German estates of his youth.[65] His descendants continued the tradition, adding plants and lawn sculpture from Germany.

Victorians were outwardly enthusiastic about the fast pace of technical progress. Beneath the surface, however, lay the worry that important values were being lost in the rush. One way to remedy that loss was to renew their contact with nature, and a garden was seen as the ideal place. Here was nature at its best—controlled, orderly, friendly—the perfect spot to shed the cares of the world. As Mrs. Charlotte Van Cleve of Minneapolis reflected:

Sometimes when busied and perplexed with cares and wearisome duties,

I look at my plants . . . and get so filled . . . [at] such loveliness, that,

after resting a few moments, my weight of care seems lightened.[66]

Should gardeners wonder just what shape "nature" should take in their own yards, there were experts eager to tell them. One of the era's strongest voices was East Coast home and landscape designer Andrew Jackson Downing (1815-1852), author of *Theories and Practice of Landscape Gardening* and *Cottage Residences*, and founder of *Horticulture Magazine*.

Downing described three styles in landscape design. The "geometric," or old-fashioned design, characterized by regularity and symmetry, was more appropriate for public gardens and old houses.[67] His other two styles were more innovative, taking their character from nature itself. "The beautiful" emphasized flowing, graceful lines and soft surfaces, while "the picturesque" stressed irregularity and the wilder aspects of nature. The site itself should determine the landscaping style.[68]

According to Downing, the house should be located where it offered a fine vista. Paths and driveways should meander slightly to provide ample opportunities for enjoying the views created by the house and plantings. Trees might be planted singly (if they were unusual looking) or in masses, but not in a straight row. Shrubs should be grouped.[69]

Downing's influence on American landscaping was immense. His celebration of the country life struck a chord in a nation fretting over technology and crowded cities, and his cottage designs were widely circulated. [70]

Examples of Downing's principles were found throughout Minnesota. An examination of A. T. Andreas's *1874 Atlas of Minnesota* reveals numerous houses whose grounds reflect the "picturesque" and the "beautiful." In Minneapolis, Evergreen, the home of grain merchant and lumberman William S. Judd, typified local interpretation of Downing's ideas. Built about 1873, the cream-colored brick house was set on a square-block lot and

·—◆—·

The William LeDuc house and grounds, pictured in 1869, remains a highly visible landmark in Hastings, Minnesota.

surrounded with a smooth lawn, iron fence, curving drives, and graceful trees. In its day, Evergreen was often called "the most showy residence in the city."[71]

At least one Minnesota family followed Downing's suggestions exactly. William LeDuc arrived in St. Paul in 1850. In rapid succession he opened a bookstore, sold pianos, bought property, set up a law practice, and operated a flour mill. The financial panic of 1857 sidelined him for a time, but businessman that he was, LeDuc survived, later volunteering as an officer in the Union army.

LeDuc's wife was Mary Elizabeth Bronson, whom he had met at Kenyon College, stronghold of Ohio Gothic architecture. Mrs. LeDuc fancied the Gothic style illustrated in Downing's book *Cottage Residences*.[72] When planning their home, she traced the villa from Downing's frontispiece on a windowpane and reversed the image. The LeDucs built a true country estate in Hastings and landscaped it in Downing's picturesque style. The house was completed in 1864 just as LeDuc was released from the army.[73]

Incorporating Downing's ideas in their landscape plans, the LeDucs sited the house to take advantage of

Minnesota Historical Society

mature oaks on the property and placed an encircling drive that matched Downing's ideal. By 1867 LeDuc had planted a dozen evergreens, most likely spruces or pines, around the house to contrast with the rugged oaks.[74] Along the Vermillion Street side he placed deciduous trees and shrubs, including lilacs. Thick vines screened the front porch; three climbing roses were planted by the veranda. The LeDucs had indeed created a spot to enjoy a "the pure and elevating pleasures of the country."[75]

By the late twentieth century the LeDuc house, no longer occupied, was on the National Register of Historic Places, though not open to the public. Only the hardiest plants remained, a small reminder of Victorian glory days.

Downing was the most influential writer on American landscape design, but he had a succession of followers, notably Frank J. Scott, who wrote later in the century for the growing middle class. Scott's *The Art of Beautifying the Home Grounds of Small Estates* catered to families with moderate-sized lots. Nature was also Scott's guide, but not "the rudeness of Nature, rather an idealized form, one that would condense and appropriate her beauties . . . eliminate the dross . . . and give them a worthy setting."[76]

Scott emphasized that the home must be a "haven of repose" embodying "all the heart's cheer, the refined pleasures, and the beauty"[77] of life. Vines, flowers, interesting trees, shrubs, and a smooth, green lawn helped to create a peaceful setting. Scott encouraged homeowners to become familiar with shrubs and trees and their "expression." Unusual leaves, twisted branches, autumn coloring, he explained, all contributed to the expression of a particular plant.[78]

Local designers like Cyrus L. Smith of Minneapolis agreed with Scott, describing at great length tree selection and lawn care.[79] Recommended ornamentals for the front lawn included weeping mountain ash, cut-leaved birch, larch, weeping poplar, and bur oak.

For many women, the window-garden enhanced the comforts of home. As one gardener said, "where we find flowers in any abode . . . there we shall find cleanliness, and a natural refinement which prompts in making the home comfortable and attractive."[80]

Minnesotans were cheered during the long winter with green plants and blooming flowers on the window sill, often bringing in plants from the summer garden. Geraniums, begonias, ivies, petunias, roses, and fuchsias were common. Freesia, crocus, tulip, and hyacinth bulbs were "forced" to give winter bloom.

D.R. Martin

"With such provision for our window," wrote a gardener from Lynd, "it is a delightful pleasure in winter to make frequent visits to our flowers when everything without is cold and cheerless."[81]

No wonder, then, that women greeted newcomers with "slips" of plants, as Mrs. Anna Todd of St. Anthony recounted.

The . . . settlers brought slips of all kinds of houseplants which they shared with [everyone]. The windows were gay with fuchias [sic], geraniums, roses, etc. . . . All started slips under an inverted tumbler to be ready for newcomers.[82]

Gardening was not merely a respite from life's cares; indeed, it was viewed as a way to understand important values about the world. Writers of the period frequently voiced the sentiment that no gardener could be a skeptic or an evil person. The reason, explained Mrs. Van Cleve at the Minnesota State Horticultural Society's annual meeting in 1876, was plain: "There are such wonders constantly revealing themselves to [the gardener] that not only must his mind acknowledge a God in all these things, but his heart must be softened and warmed to Him."[83]

Clarence Wedge, writing in the *History of Freeborn County*, was even bolder. "And so the atheist has been as rare as the drunkard among our horticulturists," because "these men cooperated with nature to bring forth the best fruits of the earth."[84]

The garden itself was understood as a symbol of the ideal life. Speaking to state horticultural society members in 1876, Reverend J. H. Tuttle, minister of the Universalist Church in Minneapolis, explained:

It was a garden in which the first human beings were placed, and from which their first sins expelled them, and in finding his way back to the lost paradise, man must enter into the garden again, pure and beautiful as the flowers that grow there.[85]

With such a high calling, small wonder gardeners took great pains with their plants. Because she had no central heating,

Hortense Share of Rosemount carried all her houseplants to the cellar each night, so as not to find them frozen stiff next morning.[86] Fannie O'Brien, of St. Paul's West Side, took horse and buggy to the woods to dig whips of elms and maples to plant in large rows around her house.[87] One would be mistaken to assume these were people with little else to do. Mrs. Share, a busy farm wife, baked forty loaves of bread a week and prepared meals for the farm hands, besides caring for her 25- by 30-foot flower garden.[88]

Despite their labors, or perhaps because of them, gardeners expressed great affection for their flowers and trees. Hortense Share called them "my pets."[89] Charlotte Van Cleve talked of "my precious calla, now blooming in all her queenly purity in my window."[90] Orchardist R. C. Cady of Freeborn County was remembered for talking about his grafting work, "with his arm around one of his trees, patting it lovingly as he talked, as if it were a child."[91]

Victorians cherished the unusual as well as the familiar. Gardens, in their infinite adaptability, satisfied both loves. By the 1870s gardeners were seeking out rare and exotic plants for their collections.

By the bay window, one might find "an Orange or Lemon tree,

Minnesota Historical Society

Gardener Charlotte Van Cleve in 1899 on her eightieth birthday.

an Oleander, Abutilon, or stately Calla,"[92] along with the geraniums and ivies. For those of means, greenhouses or conservatories expanded the repertoire of plants grown indoors. Mrs. Van Cleve described a winter visit to a neighbor's greenhouse in 1876.

I found myself, as if by magic, in the midst of lovely flowers and tropical foliage, where the air was soft and warm, the sun shone brightly, and summer reigned in wonderful beauty. Bright crimson and creamy white camelias [sic] opened their lovely cups among dark, glossy foliage, exquisite carnations bent low their fringed petals, heavy with aromatic fragrance; the slender passion vine looked in and out on pretty primroses of various hues.[93]

Outdoors, plants of the tropics began to appear. Flowering annuals such as carnations, ageratum, heliotrope, and cannas, and plants with striking foliage, including caladiums, dusty miller, coleus, alternanthera, and castor oil beans, were set in formal patterns.[94] Some plantings, called *carpet bedding*, imitated Turkish rugs, maps, medallions, and the like. Plants placed in contrasting strips along paths and drives were called *ribbon bedding. Parterres* were gardens in which beds and paths were laid out in an intricate geometric arrangement; they were designed to be viewed from the home's second-story window.

Because intricate patterns were time-consuming and difficult to maintain, they were typically found in public parks or on the grounds of well-to-do families. In fact, a complicated scheme became a status symbol. In the late 1880s many wealthy families adopted the fad with enthusiasm, spelling out the family monogram or initials in flowers. H. L. Fletcher, C. A. Pillsbury, William D. Washburn, and Colonel William King, all of Minneapolis, laid out elaborate landscape designs.[95]

·—◆—·

Indoor gardens were an integral part of Victorian gardening. These unidentified women are standing in the midst of a tropical paradise about 1895.

A number of items besides plants began to find their way onto the lawn. Cast-iron and rattan lawn furniture, large vases, cast-iron animals of all kinds, gazebos, and trellises shared space with the lilacs. For the affluent, fountains added an exciting dimension to the grounds.

By the 1880s, when Minnesota's cities were booming, wealthy citizens lavished enormous amounts of effort and money on their gardens. Milling, lumber, and railroad magnate William D. Washburn hired a team of gardeners to maintain his Minneapolis estate, Fair Oaks.[96] The grounds, which included a greenhouse, pond, and rustic bridge, were said to have been laid out by Frederick Law Olmsted, the designer of New York's Central Park.

Washburn's neighbor and business partner, Dorilus Morrison, spent almost eight hundred dollars (a tremendous sum at the time) to have his garden designed and planted. In 1892 his home, Villa Rosa, at 24th Street and 3rd Avenue in Minneapolis, was the scene for a glamorous Rose Fete, so newsworthy that the *Minneapolis Tribune* covered the event in detail.

At 3 o'clock in the afternoon a burst of music from an orchestra concealed behind a screen of shrubs and fir trees announced the opening of the floral fete at Villa Rosa. . . . The broad drive sweep was flanked at the entrance by huge bronze vases, filled with century plants and blossoms. . . . The host and hostess . . . stood on bright colored rugs beneath the branching elms immediately before the house. . . . Tiny flower laden donkeys [with] rose-decked heads [carried] golden paniers filled . . . with roses, crimson, yellow, pink and white. . . . Mrs. Morrison . . . selected [from the donkeys] a Mermet rose, and the little animals were taken . . . to every lady present till each had chosen . . . her own particular, favorite rose. . . . The fountains splashed in the distance.[97]

Morrison's fantastic garden of 1892 seems light-years away from Henchen's simple but fruitful spot. But the contrast was not lost on gardeners of the time; frequently they called for a return to simplicity and unsophisticated beauty. In 1898 Charlotte Van Cleve wistfully recalled the "Old-Time Flower Gardens" where the "walks from gate to door were bordered by a variety of colored beauties, [and] morning-glories ran riot over our fences." There, thought Van Cleve and others, were gardens that could "exert a good influence . . . unostentatiously."[98]

These traditional spots were not completely gone, as Charlotte feared. Instead, they survived in the gardens of old-fashioned people throughout Minnesota. No doubt, Van Cleve would have been at home on the grounds of St. Cloud's Elizabeth Mitchell. Grandmother Mitchell, wife of merchant and public servant Henry, gardened at 509 First Avenue from the 1860s until her death in 1910. Her grandchildren recalled "Grandmother's chief delight."

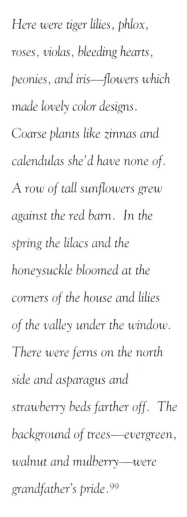

Here were tiger lilies, phlox, roses, violas, bleeding hearts, peonies, and iris—flowers which made lovely color designs. Coarse plants like zinnas and calendulas she'd have none of. A row of tall sunflowers grew against the red barn. In the spring the lilacs and the honeysuckle bloomed at the corners of the house and lilies of the valley under the window. There were ferns on the north side and asparagus and strawberry beds farther off. The background of trees—evergreen, walnut and mulberry—were grandfather's pride.[99]

The Dorilus Morrison house, about the turn of the century, on the present site of the Minneapolis Institute of Arts. Note the tropical plants on the lawn.

GARDENS OF THE DEAD

Burial grounds and cemeteries of all other places should show the fostering
hand of care, and the flowers and shrubs growing there are the mute
but beautiful and eloquent witness of an appreciation felt by the living
for those of kindred ties who have gone before.

St. Paul *Daily Pioneer and Democrat.*[100]

To the Victorian, the ideal cemetery design was a bright, open spot, located on the edge of town, with rolling terrain, magnificent trees, and curving drives. Henry Castle, an early Minnesota historian, explained, "The old conception of a burial ground as a place of gloom has been superseded by one more in consonance with our hopes of a blessed immortality, and the homes of our dead are given as attractive surroundings as the homes of the living."[101]

Garden cemeteries originated in 1831 with Mount Auburn Cemetery in Cambridge, Massachusetts, the first truly rural cemetery in the nation.[102] Before Mount Auburn, churchyard burial was customary. However, by the nineteenth century most East Coast graveyards had become crowded and often neglected. Out of criticism of the unattractive conditions, Mount Auburn was born.

In an unusual collaboration, the site was developed by the Massachusetts Horticultural Society along with property shareholders.[103] Even before development began, the area was noted for its beautiful, undulating terrain and the vigorous growth of its trees. Striving for what was essentially the English landscape style, designers placed paths and roads so they would conform to the topography and encouraged lot owners to decorate with the finest plants and memorials.[104] Mount Auburn was an immediate triumph, attracting streams of visitors. Traffic was so great on Sundays that only families and guests were admitted.

The success of Mount Auburn inspired other communities to develop their own rural cemeteries—Philadelphia's Laurel Hill in 1836, New York's Albany Rural Cemetery in 1841, and Spring Grove in Cincinnati in 1856.[105] Spring Grove, designed by Prussian gardener Adolph Strauch, took the notion of cemetery-as-park even further. The "lawn plan," still in favor today, was built around a naturalistic landscape.[106] The site was laid out in a predetermined plan which took precedence over individual preferences. No fences were allowed to mark off family plots, because they broke up the overall design. "The object in the lawn plan is not to define the [individual] lot," said one superintendent, "but to make it appear to the casual observer that this lot covers half the space of the section."[107]

44

Minnesota's earliest burial grounds were situated for convenience rather than beauty. Many farmers set aside small burial plots on their land; towns designated a field for the purpose. In St. Paul, Father Lucien Galtier established the city's first cemetery in 1841 on land now bounded by Kellogg, Minnesota, and Cedar streets.[108] The space was soon needed for another use, however, and the bodies were moved. Various fields were used, but they too fell to other claims.

Editors wasted no time in agitating for an appropriate site. In 1851 John P. Owens of the *Minnesotian* declared that "it is an utter disgrace to St. Paul, that with all her spirit of improvement and public enterprise, we have no place to bury the dead. The tract of land now used for a burial place is private property, and liable to be sold for other purposes at any moment."[109]

In response, a committee of St. Paul citizens studied the problem and eventually selected "forty acres of rolling oak grove nearly two miles from the river landing, far enough to be difficult of access and with little probability that the hum of industry would ever disturb its rural quiet."[110] The year was 1853; the land was at Jackson Woods, now the crowded intersection of Jackson, Magnolia, and Sylvan streets.

From the beginning the Oakland Cemetery Association upheld the ideal of a park-like space. It drew up rules concerning grave markers, monuments, and plantings of flowers, trees, and shrubs. Still, no master plan was devised, no roads built, until the 1870s when the board of trustees hired Horace William Shaler Cleveland, the foremost landscape architect of his day.[111]

Cleveland had worked with Frederick Law Olmsted and Calvert Vaux on Prospect Park in Brooklyn, and he had maintained a practice on the East Coast, laying out cemeteries, gardens, parks, and pleasure grounds. In 1869 he moved to Chicago, where he worked with great enthusiasm to apply landscape principles to the booming Midwest. In a series of pamphlets and articles he delineated his philosophies of landscape planning and design.[112] By engaging Cleveland for Oakland Cemetery, the board was hiring a master.

·—◆—·

Floral decorations and mature trees in St. Paul's Oakland Cemetery, 1911.

Cleveland's design called for maintaining the natural beauty of the Oakland site. He retained native trees—oaks, elms, and wild crab—and planned curving roads that conformed with the land's contours. Meandering paths led past contrasting vistas, enhancing the feeling of openness.[113] Cleveland's basic outline can still be seen today.

The idea of creating park-like cemeteries spread quickly across the state. In Rochester, civil engineer Colonel George Healy designed Oakwood Cemetery "in a manner of cemeteries out East, amid foliage and rustic surroundings."[114] His plan included a central fountain, varied terrain, circular drives, pleasant vistas, and flowers "delicate in size, form and color."[115] Duluth's Forest Hill, a "most beautiful and modern park cemetery," included a duck pond and mature trees.[116] Across Lake Winona lay Woodlawn, "that beautiful city of the silent."

Here the ground has been terraced and sodded, and broken into irregular forms, and in all things made to preserve its character as the dear resting-place for the weary. . . .The morning beams salute the faces of the terraces as the sun climbs the eastern sky and peers over the bluff in the Orient. The midday sun warms the cool shadiness and penetrates each leafy nook and green retreat.[117]

So beautiful was Woodlawn that it was featured in the national magazine, *The Modern Cemetery*. The author noted that the cemetery

nestled as it is in a beautiful dell . . . can hardly be excelled in natural beauty. . . . One of the greatest attractions consists in the magnificent native oaks, interspersed with maple, basswood, elm, spruce, balsam and other varieties of trees which have been planted. . . . In many of the sections the lot corners are marked with tiger lilies, iris, white day lilies, blue lilies of the valley and other beautiful varieties. . . . Ornamental beds and hardy shrubs abound; of the latter those mostly used are the Persian and white lilac, snowball, flowering almond, syringa, weigelia, spireas, and the flowering quince.[118]

Other Minnesota cemeteries, such as Mound Grove in Evansville and Lakewood in Minneapolis, were designed as sylvan parks "where the encroachments of the city would never seriously interfere."[119]

Having a beautiful burial place became a matter of civic pride. As Reverend J. H. Tuttle of Minneapolis stated at Lakewood's dedication: "A large, handsome, convenient public cemetery near every large city is a necessity. The refinement, wealth, and social condition of any city are indicated by the attention that city bestows on its cemetery."[120]

More importantly, at least to the Victorians, the cemetery site should lighten the spirit of mourners. William Stone, superintendent of Pine Grove Cemetery in Lynn, Massachusetts, explained that by keeping the grounds neat and attractive, the lawns and lots well kept, "the modern cemetery has robbed death of half its horror."[121]

Some citizens regarded the burial spot as an extension of their own gardens. Families picnicked there and strolled among the trees and graves. In 1893 Isaac Atwater wrote of Sir Joseph Frances, former New York businessman and inventor, whose wife was buried at Lakewood.

Mr. Francis is still living but quite advanced, being over 91 years old. He spends most of his time in summer sitting by his wife's tomb, and explaining to visitors points of interest about the cemetery. His own epitaph is already chiseled on a granite slab.[122]

Lakewood, Oakland, and Forest Hill were on streetcar stops to accommodate the many families who spent the day among the dead. Every spring people arrived with plants, seeds, and tools to make gardens for their loved ones, always including the departed's favorite flowers.

Cemetery managers lavished care on the grounds, believing with O. C. Simonds, influential superintendent in Chicago, that "the most beautiful cemeteries are those which are most park-like."[123] Superintendents, who often came to their positions by way of botany or landscape backgrounds, used the sites as testing grounds for exotic trees and shrubs. In 1904 Oakland's superintendent listed 140 varieties of plants on the grounds. So

filled is Lakewood with rare and beautiful specimens that for years University of Minnesota Forestry students made annual tree-identification field trips to the site.[124]

The mix of flowering plants was the subject of much debate among cemetery personnel. Some advocated perennials. Others argued for annuals, stating that "the best regulated cemeteries exclude all perennials [for then] there is no possibility of the grounds being overrun by spreading myrtle, mosses, thyme, etc."[125] One writer suggested low-growing annuals with compact flowers. "Our main-stay would be geraniums, salvias, heliotropes, lobelias, asters, verbenas, pansies, and phlox, among bloomers, and coleus, echeverias, alternanthera and feverfew for foliage beds."[126] Carpet bedding, the Victorian standby, was recommended for arrangements: stars, ovals, triangles, squares, anchors, sickles, crescents, were all acceptable, as long as the "right design [was put] in the right place."[127]

In smaller communities, citizens tended the cemeteries themselves. At Austin, land had been purchased but little done to improve the burial ground. In *The History of Mower County*, Franklyn Curtiss-Wedge wrote:

When the ladies thought it was time . . . for work on the cemetery grounds [they] invited the men to help. . . . Early in the morning on the day appointed one could see men and women carrying implements of all kinds, wending their way to the cemetery, and all day one could see men and women working, the women driving stakes, holding chains, picking brush and burning it. . . . Austin certainly looked like a deserted village that day, and the work which the ladies begun has been kept up till now we have one of the most beautiful resting places for one's loved ones "gone before."[128]

Large cemeteries hired numerous grounds workers. Oakland had a full-time gardener who lived on the premises. Besides overseeing the grounds, he and his staff maintained nine greenhouses for producing flowers and foliage plants. Demand for flowers was so great that in 1894 his greenhouses readied 64,000 plants for use on the grounds.

Operating a greenhouse was a costly and difficult proposition. Over the long Minnesota winters, men stoked fires for the coal-fed boilers throughout the day and night. Thermostats were not available, so workers had to walk the aisles hourly, checking thermometers and regulating the steam. Still, flowers were such an integral part of mourning that cemeteries were willing to take on the expense and trouble. As one writer in *The Modern Cemetery* noted:

There is scarcely a rural cemetery now worthy of the name in the West at least, that has not its greenhouse department for the growing of cut flowers, and more particularly for the preparation of all kinds of summer blooming plants to be used for the decoration of the grounds and lots in summer.[129]

Even small cemeteries like West Side Cemetery in St. Paul, pictured in 1915, had a staff organized for grounds maintenance to "show the fostering hand of care."

Another superintendent explained that flowers and plants "take away the harshness of the grave [and] smooth the way . . . for the dear departed ones."[130]

A newspaper account of Abby G. Mendenhall's funeral in 1900 touchingly demonstrates the importance of flowers and plants to the Victorians. In 1858 Abby Swift married Richard J. Mendenhall, a banker and Minneapolis's first florist. A lifelong gardener and lover of flowers, Abby often carried bouquets to the sick and sorrowing. When she died, her friends repaid the favor.

All was so beautiful at this funeral and so thoroughly in keeping with the woman's life and her desires. Of flowers there was a great profusion, not only about the bier and in the room in which the services were conducted, but all over the house. Mrs. Mendenhall, in life, had loved the timid lilies-of-the-valley, and these modest flowers were used much in the decorations. . . . In her hands were lilies and orchids, about her calm face were entwined more lilies, and on the mantel was a big bank of lilies-of-the-valley and ferns.[131]

PLEASURE GROUNDS

*Give your people more parks and your children more open play grounds away from
dusty streets and alleys, and I assure you that every little town of twelve or fifteen
hundred inhabitants will cease to be a refuge for three or four doctors.*

F. M. Dolan, read at a meeting of the Minnesota State Horticultural Society, 1903.[132]

As towns were being platted during the 1870s and 1880s, citizens urged community leaders to save room for parks and boulevards. The sell was not always easy. Most city officials recognized the benefits of open space, but they were not always willing to pay for it. In Minneapolis, for example, many feared that the city was becoming so crowded that "an open, ample breathing space is . . . already hard to find."[133] Yet, setting aside lands for gardens and parks was difficult because they did not bring an immediate return to municipal or private coffers. And, as historian Henry Castle explained, "there were numerous vacant tracts within the city limits, and the surrounding country was practically unbroken."[134]

Park supporters in rural communities could face tough arguments as well. With so much natural beauty close by, opponents said, what need was there for sylvan beauty inside

town? Some supporters recognized, however, that parks were a commercial asset, a way to attract settlers and tourists. Others realized the comfort and beauty to be found in green space. Franklyn Curtiss-Wedge, writing Winona's history, referred to

that wisdom [which] did not neglect the home necessities of broad streets, good crossings, sidewalks, and shade. When the first settlement was made at this point there was one solitary tree on the great Wabasha flat. Today, not thirty-two years later, the city . . . is literally embowered in shade and her streets and public parks and private grounds are vast reaches and masses of vivid greenness, the luxuriant foliage rustling most pleasantly in the summer south winds, and shutting out the burning glances of the midday sun, so severely felt in this high latitude.

**Restored Irvine Park with its elaborate fountain
epitomizes formal Victorian park design.**

49

Most everyone could agree on the health benefits. General C. C. Andrews, in his *History of St. Paul*, termed parks and boulevards "the lungs of the city. They are, in effect, breathing places where, without money and without price, the faint may be refreshed, where the tired and worried may take recreation, where the weary may be at rest."[136] In New Ulm, park supporter F. W. Johnson spoke of the "human need for relaxation and pleasure after the toil in factory, store, and office, amid grime, and clamor and nerve-wracking haste." He added, "The city which provides healthful recreation for its sons and daughters builds well for its future."[137]

As was true in Winona, many towns can give thanks for the generosity of early settlers who deeded park lands. Marshall's John Schutz and Charles B. Tyler gave a parcel of land to Cottonwood as a gift to the village.[138] In New Ulm, settled by the German Land Association of Minnesota, founding fathers recognized the beauty of the hills and river; in completing the city plat on April 7, 1858, they earmarked areas for market spaces, alleys, streets, public landings, and parks, stipulating that these tracts would always remain in public hands.[139]

The earliest city parks were modeled on the New England town square. Like Rice and Irvine parks in St. Paul, they often began as pastures, but soon communities began clamoring for improvements. Irvine Park is a case in point.[140] Led by Joseph Forepaugh, residents pressured the city to develop the land. In 1871 the park was graded; the job took forty-five days and a team of oxen. Two years later an iron fence was installed. In 1876 a sixty-foot-wide drive was added, and gas lamps and settees installed. Flower beds and a $900 fountain with waterspouts in the shape of dogs' heads were added in the 1880s.

By the 1970s the park was no longer the spot of Victorian beauty it had once been. But as the grand old houses in the neighborhood were restored, residents worked to return Irvine Park to its early glory. Landscape architect William Sanders redesigned the park, closely following the original concept. A new fountain was cast, similar to its predecessor, with gargoyles as water spouts. Now the scene of picnics, concerts, and weddings, the park is a fitting evocation of a gracious era.

When public funds were unavailable, energetic citizens did the job themselves. In St. Cloud, residents organized an Improvement Committee in April 1900, to beautify its library grounds and Central and Empire parks.[141] The group added shrubbery, vines, hedges, bulbs, and flowers and planted eight hundred apple trees around town. Zumbrota had J. A. Thatcher, first mayor of the village, to thank for the trees that "stand as silent sentinels" over its city park.[142]

Whether publicly or privately landscaped, Victorian parks were meant to be quiet oases in a busy world. They were planned not so much for passive recreation as for unstructured activities. Citizens could walk or bike along their paths. Children found them great places for jacks or marbles, or for wading in pools. Walking was promoted as especially restorative, and to that end, many parks were designed for promenading. Formal arrangements of flowers, exhibits of animals, fountains or small pools, and winding paths were common features.

German Park in New Ulm was typical. There, pedestrians could stroll past fountains, gazebos, formal flower gardens, and thick woods. Walkways curved through close-cropped lawns and under vine-covered trellises. Mothers could rest on benches while their children played on the broad paths. Old photos show young men lolling on the grass and young women carrying parasols. The scene was quiet, sedate, and pleasing to the eye, designed, as St. Paul Parks Superintendent Frederick Nussbaumer said, to be "restful [and] beneficial to soul and body."[143]

Levee Park in Winona was a landscape triumph and the only park of its kind along the Mississippi River. Called Winona's *pièce de résistance*—the place to which we take strangers and ask them if they ever saw anything like it,"[144] the park had geometrically patterned pathways, a grape arbor for shade, formal plantings, and a wide stone-paved river landing. Local attorney and landscape designer William A. Finkelnburg derived many of his ideas for Levee Park from his travels in Europe. As a place to visit friends or watch steamers plying the river, the spot was a favorite with locals and tourists.

E very community had its visionaries, those citizens and public servants who anticipated the town's growth and lobbied for its recreation and green-space needs. Perhaps the finest expressions of the park-making impulse could be seen in the Twin Cities area with its large and affluent population. Developing the extensive park systems of the two cities required the ardent voices of many civic leaders.

Newspaperman Joseph Wheelock of St. Paul and business leader Charles Loring of Minneapolis lobbied long and hard to acquire land for parks. Wheelock, as park commissioner and founder and editor-in-chief of the *St. Paul Press*, later the *Pioneer Press*, successfully urged citizens to plan for parks and boulevards.

Cascade Park in Duluth, as depicted on an early twentieth-century postcard, provided a quiet oasis in the midst of city bustle.

·—◆—·

Charles Loring was a retired miller when he was elected president of the first Minneapolis park board in March, 1883. During his many years on the board, he led efforts to create the city's park and boulevard system.[145] One of the board's first acts was to purchase the land for what would become Loring Park, before it was swallowed up by homes and businesses. Originally called Central Park, in 1890 the site was renamed in honor of Loring, the "Father of the Minneapolis Park System."

However, two men, by way of their positions and the times in which they served, stand out as most influential: Parks Superintendents Frederick Nussbaumer in St. Paul and Theodore Wirth in Minneapolis (see Public Efforts, Private Benefits). To their posts the men brought organizational skills, an all-encompassing view of what parks could be, and, most importantly, a fervor that enabled them to persuade others.

One of the grandest outcomes of the thrust to build parks was the glass-domed conservatory at Como Park. By 1900 crystal palaces were featured attractions at many city parks in other states, but not in Minnesota. Had it not been for the determined entreaties of Nussbaumer, St. Paul might never have had its own conservatory.

Born in Baden, Germany, where his father was a nurseryman, Nussbaumer had spent his youth working in the great gardens of Europe.[146] As a seventeen-year-old, he was employed as a gardener at London's Kew Gardens. Much was impressive about Kew, but for Nussbaumer the large, glass-domed Palm House was the *chef d'oeuvre*. Its size, beauty, and organization all remained in his memory as something he would someday want to duplicate.

After two years in London, Nussbaumer was hired by one of the largest nurseries in France, and during his stint in Paris he met Horace Shaler Cleveland, the great American landscape architect.[147] In addition to designing St. Paul's Oakland Cemetery, Cleveland had suggested a comprehensive design for the city, calling for the development of Lake Como and the riverfront. Cleveland recognized talent when he saw it, and urged Nussbaumer to ply his trade in America.

When Nussbaumer arrived in St. Paul in 1878, he discovered that Como was a park in name only.[148] Land had been set aside in 1872, but the economic crisis of 1873 had derailed all thoughts of development.

Nussbaumer first worked as a contract laborer and market gardener, eventually buying ten acres of farmland near Como Park. Finally, in 1887 the economy had improved and St. Paul established its park board, which considered developing a park around Lake Como. Nussbaumer hired on as a laborer there and soon was promoted to foreman. In 1889 he was named superintendent of St. Paul parks, a position he held until 1922.

The title was a bit misleading, explained attorney Lloyd Peabody to the Executive Council of the Minnesota Historical Society in 1913.

The park areas belonging to the old system . . . were merely a haphazard lot of open spaces, which had come to the possession of the city in all sorts of ways. . . .These areas had no relation to each other, nor to any general plan.[149]

In fact, early in its history, St. Paul's parks had been little more than cow pastures. The editor of *McClung's City Directory* for 1866 had this to say about Rice Park: "As a specimen of beauty unadorned . . . it stands unrivaled among the attractions of the city. . . . Among the rare plants, shrubs, and evergreens that annually spring spontaneously from the dust and lend their fragrance to purify the air are fox-tail, pigeon-grass, juniper weed and dog fennel." There were no deer, said the writer, but snakes, "gophers, toads, and other vermin too tedious to mention."[150]

But Nussbaumer, having seen and worked in the parks of Europe, knew what a park could be. It was a vision he shared with his friend, newspaperman Joseph A. Wheelock. As Peabody described it:

Mr. Wheelock spends the most of what to other men would have been leisure time in going about the city and its environs in company with . . . Mr. Nussbaumer, . . . planning an area here, a connecting boulevard there, and perfecting and bringing into symmetry as a whole that remarkable series of natural intervals and spaces which we now know as our park system.[151]

Nussbaumer believed that St. Paul must have a "recreation ground for all classes of people, a safe and decorous place . . . where families with children, sick or convalescent persons, the nature-loving enthusiast, and the frugal workman alike may find a visit . . . refreshing, restful, profitable, beneficial to soul and body."[152] With untiring zeal, he wrought significant changes, not only at Como, but in the park system as a whole.

In Nussbaumer's first years, his accomplishments at Como were many—the Schiffman Fountain at Circle Drive, an array of elaborate flower beds, a shrub and tree nursery, a lily pond, and the Gates Ajar display. He persuaded streetcar companies to bring a line out to the park so people could reach it easily.

In 1904 he completed the first municipal Japanese garden in Minnesota.[153] The impetus was Dr. Rudolph Schiffman's gift of a rare and large collection of Japanese shrubs and trees, purchased at the St. Louis World's Fair from the Japanese Commission. The designer, a man known only as "Itchikawa," had been a landscape architect for the Emperor of Japan.

Tall, bamboo gates opened into the three-acre garden, located where the golf course is now. Once inside, a waterfall emptied into small pools before dropping to Cozy Lake, the garden's focal point. "A wooden bridge," according to the *St. Paul Pioneer Press*, "[was] almost hidden by the low hanging boughs of cherry trees."[154]

The garden was a popular spot for years; photos show ladies and gents of the era standing on the bridge and sitting casually around the lake. Just when the garden disappeared has been lost to history. "Cozy Lake dried up. . . . The cherry trees died, the bridge was torn down," said the *Press* article in 1932.[155] By 1928 demand for a golf course caused the entire area to be cleared.

Nussbaumer's policy was always to enhance and beautify the parks, even in the face of opposition. When Summit Avenue was opened from Lexington to the Mississippi River, Nussbaumer held out for a divided, tree-lined parkway, an idea his opponents thought was impractical and silly.[156] Today, Summit Avenue is a St. Paul showpiece, giving the inner city its distinctive elegance.

The notion of a Crystal Palace seemed equally foolhardy to many, but Nussbaumer persisted, explaining that the new conservatory would "prove to be of great advantage and immeasurable benefit to the city."[157] In 1913, after twenty years of lobbying, Nussbaumer won the day; the board gave him fifty dollars to develop a set of general plans for the erection of a new greenhouse. The following year St. Paul approved a $280,000 bond issue, for constructing Como greenhouse and improving St. Paul's parks.

Though documentation is scarce, it appears that Toltz Engineering Company designed the building, with a great deal of input from Nussbaumer.[158] King Construction Company of Tonawando, New York, handled the construction for $58,825.

Como Conservatory (pictured in an early photo, left) opened its doors to the public on Sunday, November 7, 1915, greeting the three thousand visitors with a splendid chrysanthemum display and an orchestral concert. The magnificent sixty-four-foot glass-domed Palm House was flanked by identical wings, the Sunken Garden and the North House, each twenty-six feet wide and one hundred feet long. Lush tropical foliage stretched toward the glass ceilings. Nussbaumer was on hand to point out features of the building and the collections.[159]

"Second to none in both size and appointments,"[160] the Crystal Palace drew excited crowds from the beginning. Within three years more than 77,500 plants were growing under glass, making the building a showcase for a botanical collection of plants.[161] With the conservatory, Nussbaumer put the crowning touch on St. Paul's parks, holdings which could now in truth be called a "system."

GREAT ESTATES

&

PASSIONATE

GARDENERS

Early 20th Century

—◆—

The teahouse and pergola at Mayowood are relics of grander days.

Eugene O'Neill

GRAND & GLORIOUS

Fred Stoltenberg, manager of the Mayowood Greenhouses, has gone to Europe
for the purpose of collecting new specimens of plants for the Rochester greenhouse.
He will visit several famous gardens in Germany, France, Spain, and
Italy to gather botanical specimens to be brought back here.

Rochester Post-Bulletin, July 22, 1925.[162]

Minnesota's economy was flourishing in the early twentieth century. The population, fueled by new arrivals of immigrants, jumped from 1,310,283 in 1890 to 2,075,708 twenty years later. Flour milling in the south, lumbering along the eastern border, and iron mining in the north brought prosperity to many and great fortunes to an enterprising and lucky few.

By the late 1800s families of means were heading for the suburbs to escape the dirt and clamor of the city. The building boom was on in the lake districts of Minneapolis, the East End in Duluth, and Crocus Hill in St. Paul. James J. Hill, the railroad tycoon, built his mansion on St. Paul's Summit Avenue. Frank B. Forman erected an enormous Classical Revival house on the eastern shore of Lake Calhoun. In describing the Forman property, *The Western Architect* mentioned "an attractive pavilion near the main entrance to the grounds . . . with marble statuary, griffins, settees, etc., besides the formal gardens, fountains, trees and shrubbery."

The estate was especially fine, the editor thought, because it gave "the owner all the benefits of a country place with easy reach of business."[163]

As the new century dawned, more and more affluent citizens moved to sylvan retreats just outside the city—the eastern shores of Lake Superior near Duluth and Lake Minnetonka west of Minneapolis. The exodus to Wayzata and White Bear began as a search for summer homes, but the areas soon became year-round residences for many. These lavish country homes, buffered on all sides by vast acreage, were typically patterned after European models, often English Tudor or Italian villa.

Wealthy Minnesotans traveled abroad, returning with furniture, art, china—and ideas. Dr. Charles H. Mayo came

Gardens, like that of Minneapolis's E. G. Walton at 802 Mount Curve Avenue in 1915, were increasingly splendid.

the cape of a Spanish priest.[164] The Chester Congdons of Duluth brought back European landscape paintings and oriental rugs. Mrs. Congdon collected fine laces and information about gardens.[165] Country estates, as a result, were a fantastic blend of periods and regions. An English border garden did not seem out of place beside an Italian pergola; a Japanese moon-gate opened onto a geometric parterre.

Minnesota Historical Society, Kenneth Clark III

home from his yearly trips to Europe or the Orient bringing a Japanese teahouse, French antiques, and objects that had once belonged to Napoleon; a trip to Mexico yielded art treasures and

·——◆——·

*The garden of George F. Lindsey at 294 Summit, St. Paul, about 1922 was planned on a grand scale—
formal design, statuary, privacy wall, and pool.*

And what grand places they were. Highcroft, the Lake Minnetonka country home of Frank H. Peavey, the flour-milling magnate, was built on an open plateau and set against a backdrop of ancient maple and linden trees. Original plans for the grounds were prepared by Frederick Law Olmsted of Boston, but brought to completion by Warren Manning. Manning's projects included the Chicago World's Fair of 1893, several large city park systems, and private estates. His design for Highcroft included a seven-acre front lawn, views of Lake Minnetonka and surrounding meadows, and a tree-lined drive. On the south end of the house he placed a sunken formal garden. Enormous trees, many six to nine inches in diameter, were transplanted onto the property.[166] The grand estate endured until 1952 when it was dismantled to make room for an elementary school.

Another vanished glory is Villa Emile and its surrounding acreage on Coney Island in Clearwater Lake. In its day, the island off Waconia was a favorite summering ground for entrepreneurs from around the region. The most colorful character was Emile Amblard, a dashing Frenchman who spent twenty lively years developing his part of the island.

Born in Paris in 1840, Amblard was the son of a wealthy landowner and mayor of Perigueux. After an education in Paris and a stint in the Franco-German War, he traveled the world representing Chauvenet Wine, introducing "still" and "sparkling" burgundy to the American market. In 1890 Amblard's old friend Rudolph Steinmetz, formerly of Germany and later a resident of Minneapolis, took him on a fishing trip to Clearwater Lake. Amblard was immediately attracted to the area and in 1893 purchased property there.

While on business in Canada in 1894, Amblard met and married Mary Augusta Wood, the twenty-two-year-old daughter of the late Chief Justice of Manitoba, the Honorable E. B. Wood. From then until Amblard's death in 1914, the couple spent summers on the island.

Rich, handsome, and charismatic, Amblard cut a romantic figure in a community of solid German citizens. He lavished money and energy on his country estate, adding improvements to the house and grounds every summer.[167]

He designed the buildings and landscaping with no concern for cost. On the western end of the island, Amblard created a large park, laced through with winding paths and exotic shrubs and flowers. During the last year of his life, Amblard opened a portion of the park to the public. Charles A. Reid, editor of the *Waconia Patriot*, reported:

[I was] highly pleased and impressed with the artistic layout of the many avenues lined with cobblestones, magnificent flowers beds, native and foreign shrubbery, gigantic trees under which can be found rest places with chairs and tables and swings, and at higher points . . . the large pavilions or "lookouts" from which one can enjoy the beautiful surroundings at the best of advantage.[168]

After her husband's death in 1914, Mary Amblard sold the estate to hotel interests and the property changed hands several times. Like all untended gardens, Amblard's became, over time, a haven for brush and trees. Today, there is no indication of the cultivated beauty he loved.

Considering the transitory nature of gardens, it is amazing to find any that have survived from the early twentieth century. Two that have, though in somewhat altered form, are open for visitors.

Once grand and glorious, the gardens of Dr. Charles H. and Edith Graham Mayo at Mayowood, just outside of Rochester, still retain a taste of their former luster. The Mayo brothers, easy-going C.H. and the reserved William, founded the Mayo Clinic. World-famous surgeons, the men developed the first integrated private group practice and later the Mayo Foundation for Medical Education and Research. The brothers entertained frequently and their patients included the rich and famous from around the world.

In 1893 Dr. Charlie married Edith Graham, Rochester's first trained nurse. Through their early years, they lived in town on Southwest Fourth Street. But with eight children and a steady stream of visitors, their house must have seemed inadequate.

Mr. and Mrs. Emile Amblard and Mrs. Amblard's mother, Mrs. E.B. Wood, relax on Coney Island in front of an enormous bed of cannas.

Remembering vividly her own childhood on the farm, Edith Mayo suggested building a rural retreat—a place healthy for their growing children and an escape from the pressures of C.H.'s professional life. Dr. Charlie quickly agreed, and the family selected a tract of rolling hillside and dense woodlands where they frequently picnicked. The site, then five miles out of town, was around their favorite oak tree.

Mayo designed the fifty-five-room house himself. No plans seem to have been drawn up; instead, Charlie commandeered the contractor working on brother Will's house and explained what he wanted.[169] Completed in 1911, the massive villa of stone, poured concrete, and tile is situated on a high ridge overlooking the Zumbro River. Eventually, the house was part of a three-thousand-acre estate that included eight farms, a harness-racing track, a man-made lake, extensive gardens, and a greenhouse with discarded glass X-ray plates for its roof.[170]

Once the house was finished, Dr. Charles turned to developing agriculture and beautifying the grounds. The national park movement was in full swing, and concern for the environment was widespread. During his presidency (1901-1909), Theodore Roosevelt had created fifty-three wildlife preserves across the nation. Minnesotans, too, rallied round wilderness conservation groups. Watching millions of acres of pine forest turned into board feet of lumber, they began to call for protection of the remaining forests. In 1902 the Minnesota National Forest (now called Chippewa) was established near Bemidji.[171]

A strong supporter of conservation, C. H. Mayo kept a large portion of his acreage in trees and underbrush. When neighboring properties were about to be developed, he bought up the land and left it as woodland. Declaring Mayowood a game refuge, he brought in flocks of Canada geese and deer from the Orient.[172]

The farm was always an important, though perhaps not a revenue-producing part, of the estate. Besides the horses, C. H. maintained a model dairy operation and raised poultry, cattle, and hogs. He was fond of entering his animals at the state fair and could frequently be found talking with one of the neighboring farmers.

·——◆——·

Dr. Charlie Mayo's greenhouse in Rochester in 1925.

Edith teased him about the farm's productivity, but he replied: "I am not a farmer; I am an agriculturist. The agriculturist makes his money in town and spends it on the farm; while the farmer makes his money on the farm, and spends some of it in town."[173]

Dr. Charlie's heart may have been in farming, but a significant chunk of his energy went into his gardens. Just as he built the house without formal plans, C. H. seems to have approached the gardens without detailed designs. Adding a pond here or a bridge there, over time the Mayos created a splendid array of gardens. Often, the inspiration for a new space came from an object they had picked up overseas.[174]

Besides the usual fruit and vegetable plots, the Mayos had a hillside of perennials, a field of blue flowers for Edith, and a Japanese garden that stretched across a string of small islands in a lake, which C. H. created by damming the Zumbro River. Stone lanterns and fountains decorated the islands. Drives around the estate were lined with hand-laid limestone walls, inspired by similar fences in Scotland and Ireland. Off the wing of the "Big House," a vine-covered pergola led to the teahouse bordered with perennials.

C. H. also installed a series of cascading ponds, which dropped in steps from the house to the river below. The concrete pools, some of them enormous, were stocked with Japanese carp and kept in operation all winter.

Dr. Charlie fancied chrysanthemums. With the help of his horticulturist Fred Stoltenberg, formerly professor at the University of North Dakota, C. H. raised over 165 varieties, hybridized several new ones, and orchestrated the yearly mum display in his greenhouse. In 1924 the *Rochester Post Bulletin* reported that between thirteen and fourteen thousand people attended the chrysanthemum show, the "largest of its kind in the country outside of New York and Tacoma, Washington."[175] Bus loads left the Rochester depot on the half-hour to bring in visitors. Besides the sixty thousand mums on view, the exhibit included "a number of poinsettias, begonia, calendulas . . . carnations, rubrum lilies, cyclamen, snap dragons, Jerusalem cherries and English telegraph cucumbers. "[176]

The greenhouse was festooned with Japanese lanterns and converted into a Japanese garden for the duration of the show. Mrs. C. H. Mayo was on hand to christen a new brown pom pom variety of chrysanthemum developed at the greenhouse during the previous year. It was named "Little Fred" after Mrs. Mayo's grandson.[177]

Exuberant, spontaneous, and extensive, the gardens were an accurate expression of the Mayos' spirit. They were also labor-intensive—made possible by the cheap labor available at the time. Rumor has it that at one point Dr. Charles had sixty men working on the farms and grounds; he could hire a worker for room and board and perhaps a dollar a day.[178]

After C. H.'s death in 1939, his son Charles William (Dr. Chuck) inherited Mayowood and a changed economic climate. World War II and post-war prosperity were the beginning of the end for many gardens. Payroll taxes, higher wages, and a reduced pool of workers—all made upkeep impossible. Gradually, the distant gardens on the island began to fade; silt started filling the lake. In the 1950s and 1960s the Mayos began selling off the farms. The flood of 1978 carried off the remaining structures on the islands.

In 1965 Dr. Chuck Mayo and his wife Alyse gave their home and ten acres to the Olmsted County Historical Society. During the first fifty days in 1966 that Mayowood was open to the public, 1,300 visitors came to look.[179] In the years since, visitors have continued to stream in to see this relic of grander days. The house has been kept in excellent form, and though not as complete as when Dr. Charlie and Edith lived there, the grounds still offer much to enjoy. The pergola and teahouse afford a fine view of the site, climbing roses and clematis scale the walls, and annuals and perennials grow around the manor, maintained by the Friends of Mayowood Residence and the Rochester Garden and Flower Club. Dreams for the future include the restoration of the gardens to their original splendor.

The Chester Congdons of Duluth might have been horrified at the Mayos' casual approach to building. They were meticulous people who attended to every detail of construction, and their architect and landscape engineer were of the same mind.[180] Glensheen, their thirty-nine-room mansion, was possibly the finest home in northeastern Minnesota.

All this luxury seemed remote in 1880, when Chester Congdon wrote to his fiancee Clara Hespera Bannister that "maybe I'm nothing more than a second rate lawyer and certainly I should have the good sense to be a cowboy on the plains."[181] He estimated his net worth as "$9.67 in cash, $5 received from his law firm, a month's prepaid rent at $8, a meal ticket of $5.75, two pounds of crackers, two pounds of canned meat and one half pound of coffee."[182] Fifteen years later he was on his way to becoming one of the richest men in Minnesota.

Clara and Chester, children of Methodist ministers, met at Syracuse University in the 1870s. They agreed to marry, but delayed wedding plans until Chester was suitably employed. Congdon came west to seek his fortune, taught school for a year in Wisconsin, then moved to St. Paul where he studied for and passed the bar exam. It was then that he wrote Clara of his meager assets; she had waited four years in Syracuse.[183]

A year later, in 1881, Congdon's fortunes began to change when he met W. W. Billson, U. S. Attorney for the State of Minnesota, who asked him to become his assistant. Word was sent to Clara to prepare for a wedding.

Clara and Chester lived in St. Paul until 1892, when Billson, now in private practice, moved to Duluth and brought Congdon into his law firm. Duluth's business life was soaring. James Scott, author of *Duluth's Legacy*, described the era this way: "Between 1889 and 1892 the docks, sawmills and warehouses poured forth shingles, doors, boards and ties to near and distant markets. In 1887 the major market was the Twin Cities. By 1900 the market was nationwide."[184] In Duluth, Congdon became legal counsel to Henry Oliver, developer of the steel industry on the Mesabi Range. His work for Oliver brought overlooked mining land to his attention, land that was to make him a millionaire. Together, Oliver and Congdon formed the Chemung Iron Company to mine low-grade ore. At age forty-eight Congdon had taken the step that would make him wealthy.

By 1905 Chester was ready to build his estate, to construct his legacy. He hired Clarence H. Johnston, Sr., a St. Paul architect who received numerous state commissions. For the grounds, he retained Charles Leavitt, a civil and landscape engineer with experience in the East. In their thorough fashion, the Congdons and the architects met for two years before actual construction began. The site was a gentle slope on Lake Superior between two creeks; the architectural style was Jacobean Revival.

A formal house and garden tucked between woods and water, the completed manor was a wonderful blending of site and

·—◆—·

This 1930s stereopticon shows Glensheen in its prime; terraces led from the Congdons' mansion down toward Lake Superior. Inset: Chester Congdon in 1916.

structures. In keeping with Chester Congdon's love of nature, Leavitt kept much of the original vegetation: birch, maple, and spruce remained, interwoven with trails.[185] Bent Brook was lined with stones to control erosion. Along Tischer Creek he placed a stone arch bridge and massive stepping stones for crossings. The main driveway followed the natural contours of the land, creating an S-shaped approach. To minimize their encroachment on the environment, Leavitt placed all utilities underground. So carefully did everything proceed that the building site escaped the usual baldness and devastation during construction.[186]

Formal gardens were planted around a series of terraces leading from the mansion down the slope towards Lake Superior. Brick pathways and walls, rectangular patches of lawn, and linear hedges provided structure and symmetry. Loose profusions of flowers added color and fluid lines. In the borders grew masses of traditional perennials—delphiniums, phlox, roses, coral bells, iris, and clematis. Bulging pots of lobelia, alyssum, and geraniums decorated the balustrades. On the lower terrace, a reflecting pool and fountain formed a centerpiece. Itemizing the trees, shrubs, perennials, vines, ferns, grasses, and roses for the estate, Leavitt listed 266 plants.[187]

Jay Steinke

64

Both Clara and Chester were involved in planning the garden. Clara, an amateur painter, no doubt added ideas on color and design. Chester was interested in the trees and overall appearance of the site. A 1910 trip to the famous gardens of Hampton Court in England prompted these notes in Chester's memorandum book:

Salvia (red) with mallow in bed, bordered with golden treasure fuchsia makes good bed. Best bed is double pink begonia mixed with border of Leucophytou [sp.] Browni . . . White flowered potato climber . . . Wife says we have it—Marjorie [daughter] says no.[188]

In 1915 Clara's clear handwriting records the order of twenty-six roses from a Baltimore Nursery. Among the ones she selected were the classically beautiful Baroness Rothschild, Mrs. John Laing, and Gloire de Lyonnaise.[189]

Glensheen was designed to be a self-sufficient estate with pastures and barns for cows and horses. Separate plots and an orchard supplied fresh fruit and vegetables. Two large greenhouses nurtured roses and carnations for year-round floral arrangements, and Easter lilies and poinsettias in season. A third, the Palm House, grew exotic fruit and orchids. Yet another warmed young tomato plants and annual bedding plants—zinnias, cosmos, marigolds, and geraniums.[190] Clay tennis courts and a bowling green afforded recreation. A brick cottage housed the gardener and his family.

In a rare example of continuity, the Congdon estate retained the same gardening family for over sixty years. George Wyness, with his wife Cora and three sons, came to Glensheen in 1921 as the estate's third head gardener.[191] Today, their youngest son Robert remains in the gardener's cottage, retired from active duty as head gardener since 1985, but still a vital link with Glensheen's past.

George Wyness brought distinguished experience when he arrived in Minnesota, having worked for Lord Keith on the Usan Estate in Montrose, Scotland, and for Henry Frick, chairman of the board for Carnegie Steel and Coke Business. At Frick's estate on the coast near Boston, Wyness oversaw construction of the mansion and gardens.

At Glensheen, George maintained the flower and vegetable gardens, the orchard, and four greenhouses. The task was enormous. Each fall he readied cuttings of two hundred and fifty geraniums for the following summer and grew the seedlings of flowers and vegetables. Every spring he and two assistants set out 6,000 small plants in the Glensheen gardens. George, and later Robert, kept a daily journal of garden activities and the condition of the grounds. Tending the greenhouses was no small job. Merely watering the plants by hand took two and a half hours; keeping the furnace stoked on cold nights required constant vigilance.[192]

Chester Congdon died in 1916, only eight years after Glensheen was completed, but Clara continued to live on the estate until her death in 1950 at ninety-six. The family gave the mansion and twenty-two acres to the University of Minnesota in 1968, with the provision that Clara's daughter Elisabeth might remain there as long as she lived. Since July, 1979, when the estate was opened to the public, Glensheen mansion and the gardens have been a popular stop for tourists.[193]

The gardens have not remained static during their ninety-year history, of course. Nature has taken care of that. But because they have received constant nurturing from the Congdons, the Wynesses, and since 1985, Dan McClelland, staff horticulturist and landscape architect, the grounds remain in superb condition.

Many of the original plants continue to thrive. The Japanese tree lilacs in the east court have grown as tall as the forty-two-foot house. The present potted bay trees bordering the terrace were grown from cuttings of the original 1908 trees. Each year the gardener stores them in the root cellar for the winter.[194] Old-fashioned perennials—phlox, foxglove, and delphiniums—are still flourishing. The plan that Charles Leavitt and the Congdons so carefully devised has proved enduring. Even the meticulous Chester would be pleased.

•——◆——•

Fine, consistent care has enabled the gardens of Glensheen to remain as lovely today as they were sixty years ago.

Following page: The formal garden of businessman Paul Watkins of Winona in 1932.

PRIVATE EFFORTS, PUBLIC BENEFITS

The old standards common to city and country and to all men alike have been displaced by higher standards, and more important still is the enthusiasm of civic endeavor.

Henry Castle, *History of St. Paul and Vicinity*, 1912.[195]

The early years of the twentieth century provided many Minnesotans with a bit of breathing space. The country was at peace and economically stable. Communities had grown beyond their raw pioneer status and had well-established churches and schools. Homesteaders had often become farmers or shopkeepers. Some families had resided in Minnesota for several generations and held positions of influence. In towns around the state, people began to reappraise their neighborhoods and communities. They saw a pattern of helter-skelter growth, with no serious forethought or planning. The bare necessities were in place, but none of the amenities.

In unprecedented numbers, groups and individuals favored some form of aesthetic betterment for their communities. The movement, known nationally as City Beautiful, was inspired by the classic architecture and axial arrangement of the streets and gardens of the 1893 World's Columbian Exposition in Chicago. City Beautiful had a lasting impact on towns and cities across the United States.[196] Over twenty-seven million people (one in every five Americans) attended the Exposition. Many were from small Minnesota towns. To visitors accustomed to the dirt and disarray of their own towns and farms, the event's "White City" was dazzling.[197]

In his autobiography, *A Son of the Middle Border*, Hamlin Garland described the reaction of his parents, who came from their Dakota farm to the exposition:

Stunned by the majesty of the vision, my mother sat in her chair, visioning it all yet comprehending little of its meaning. Her life had been spent among homely small things, and these gorgeous scenes dazzled her, overwhelmed her, letting in upon her in one mighty flood a thousand stupefying suggestions of the art and history and poetry of the world. At last utterly overcome she leaned her head against my arm, closed her eyes and said, "Take me home. I can't stand any more of it."[198]

The City Beautiful movement arrived in Minnesota between 1900 and 1910. In its grandiose form, it encouraged large-scale civic improvements such as municipal art, impressive architecture, and city planning. McMillan Plaza at the Capitol in Washington, D. C., is a famous example.

But small, piecemeal projects were important as well. An attractive city, proponents claimed, could improve the local economy as well as boost town pride. Boulevard tree-planting, front-yard flower contests, and funding for park band shells were but a few of the enterprises sparked by the movement.[199] Whether prompted by City Beautiful rhetoric or not, Minnesotans made valuable contributions, often with meager budgets, toward upgrading their communities.

As St. Paul historian Henry Castle explained in 1912: "More and more American cities are beginning a new life. . . . Men and women have learned that they are responsible for their city and can make it what they will." Women, he asserted, were "the natural leaders for the realization of the city beautiful," because they "have always set the moral and esthetic standard in the community in which they lived. Once [they] get into this new field . . . they ought to accomplish wonders."[200]

Castle was talking about women in St. Paul, but he could just as well have been describing Anna B. Underwood of Lake City. She and a group of "earnest women" organized in the early 1900s to beautify their town. The reason: "Although nature had done much for [the town] in the way of a most beautiful lake, surrounded by picturesque bluffs and valleys . . . there was much found to offend the sight."[201] Mrs. Underwood mentioned unkempt yards and unattractive streets as immediate problems. "We had no funds," she continued in a report before the Minnesota State Horticultural Society in 1906, "only plenty of talk and a reasonable degree of influence."[202] It proved to be sufficient.

Anna Bingham Underwood, wife of leading horticulturist and nurseryman Joseph M. Underwood, was in a good position to press her case. Her husband owned Jewell Nursery, was president of the Minnesota State Horticultural Society, and mayor of Lake City. Anna was a member of the Daughters of the American Revolution, the Order of the Eastern Star, and a life member of the Minnesota Horticultural Society.

Minnesota Historical Society

Not only was Anna a student of botany and a practical and interested gardener, but "she brought to her garden new and rare plants and trees, many of which are now common in Minnesota dooryards."[203] She had read the national magazine *Garden and Forest*, and agreed with the editor that "trees and shrubs and flowers and grasses are possessions of as real and practical value as are pure water, good drainage, fresh air, hospitals, schools and churches."[204]

Accordingly, Underwood and her committee organized a flower-planting campaign in the summer of 1905. Working through the Lake City school, they distributed free packets of seeds—morning glories, sweet alyssum, four-o'clocks, nasturtiums, calendulas, and zinnias. In all, 244 children joined the "Flower Band," planting seeds in their yards. Local newsmen followed the program eagerly, reporting on the "first" and "best" flowers. In August the committee's much-touted Flower Carnival, with plant displays and booths selling Russian tea, cake, and ice cream, netted eighty dollars and "a whole lot of enthusiasm and courage."[205]

Emboldened, the Improvement Club, as the women now called themselves, tackled increasingly larger projects. In addition to the annual flower-planting contest, they sodded and beautified the school grounds. Noticing the sad state of land just past the train depot, they added ornamental trees and herbaceous plants, a fountain, and goldfish. In its third season (1908) the Improvement Club discovered a Minnesota state law that authorized a park board for towns with populations under ten thousand; Lake City had about half that number. The club persuaded the town to create such a board, assuring a public voice for parks and recreation areas.[206] In the club's fifth season, the street committee, comprised of "three successful businessmen [who] worked as though they were drawing a large salary instead of much criticism,"[207] graded and improved city streets.

•—◆—•

Anna Underwood, photographed in 1884, was an energetic beautifier of Lake City.

Improvement Club members noted that a spruced-up park or a neatly kept lawn inspired nearby residents to "brace up and take notice" so their own yards presented a neat and tidy appearance.[208]

After several successful years the group that started with no budget found that it was "so much easier to press [its] claims now than six years ago, especially as we can point to what we have already accomplished."[209]

Lyceum President John H. Rich called for a Civic League which would be responsible for beautification of the streets. Organized one month later, the group's mission was to "improve and beautify our city and make it more desirable as a place of residence."[211] Rich, Densmore, and merchant George H. Cook, owner of the Golden Rule Department Store, took a strong interest from the beginning, leading numerous improvement campaigns in Red Wing.

Red Wing's Levee Park (shown above in a period postcard) owes its existence to the City Beautiful spirit. At a 1903 meeting of the Red Wing Lyceum, Frances Densmore, later famous for her work in ethnic music, made a speech about building a carriage road to scenic Barn Bluff. Incidentally, she mentioned improving the appearance of several unsightly areas of town, especially the waterfront.[210]

"At the time," wrote Franklyn Curtiss-Wedge in his history of Goodhue County, "Red Wing was like many other cities of the same size—trees disfigured with posters and signs, empty lots and yards grown to weeds, sidewalks and streets littered with filth and rubbish, and its one park in a state of sad neglect."[212]

In John Rich, the Civic League had an able and energetic leader. An entrepreneur who was "associated with a great number

John Rich Park in downtown Red Wing is a legacy of early beautification efforts.

·—◆—·

of Red Wing's large successful enterprises"[213] (he was president of the Red Wing Sewer Pipe Company, the Red Wing Malting Company, the Goodhue County National Bank, and the Forest Products Company), Rich always found time to devote much of his energy to the public welfare.

The Civic League's initial project was overhauling the levee, important because it was the first glimpse of the city for many visitors. A run-down depot, dilapidated buildings, and debris-strewn vacant lots were an embarrassment to Red Wing. Moving swiftly, the League persuaded city officials to approve the project. By spring of 1906 the city had a new concrete levee wall, a stone-faced depot (funded by the Chicago, Milwaukee and St. Paul Railroad), and a park designed by William A. Finkelnburg of Winona.

Arbor Day was set as the official planting day. Citizens dug trees from their own yards to be placed in the park. Civic organizations gave money. Fourteen hundred school children donated small coins to help purchase trees and later helped to plant them. The *Red Wing Daily Republican* described the scene:

The lower grades held the fort first. With their teachers the little tots marched to the river front. . . . Twenty-three trees were planted. They consisted of white birch, mountain ash, hard maple and elm. These trees were paid for by the children themselves. . . . The little ones looked on in astonishment. . . . They knew that they had helped to make Red Wing's Levee park.[214]

Seventy-five trees were planted, including elms, hackberries, and butternuts, in addition to a long hedge of flowering shrubs to separate the park from the railroad tracks. Paths and flower beds were laid.

Over the next few years, stirred to civic pride by the League, Red Wing citizens improved public and residential spaces.

Mr. Cook himself planted Virginia Creeper around nearly every store and brick building in Red Wing and arranged flower and vegetable contests among the children. In 1909 banker and bookstore owner A. W. Pratt organized a *bee* of "business men and on a day now historic, the stores all closed, a band discoursed music, while the business and professional men of Red Wing donned overalls and built a path"[215] to the top of Barn Bluff overlooking the Mississippi River. Downtown, John Rich turned the waste space between East and West avenues into a beautifully landscaped entryway.

Red Wing had discovered the strength of mobilizing interest throughout the community. According to area newspapers—in Eau Claire, New Ulm, and Menominee—Red Wing's "young people and the old joined hands, and [with] the planning of the old people and the working of the young . . . have done much to make Red Wing—'The Desirable City.'"[216]

Not all community projects were prompted by City Beautiful ideology. Certainly, Eloise Butler's campaign for a wildflower garden stemmed from other motives. Interestingly, the twenty-two-acre preserve she founded and developed in Minneapolis, now called the Eloise Butler Wildflower Garden and Bird Sanctuary, boosted city pride and the local economy just as surely as Levee Park did for Red Wing.

When Eloise arrived in Minneapolis in 1877 as a teacher, she brought with her sweet memories of tramping the bogs, forests, and meadows of her native Maine. She later wrote that her "chief amusement" in childhood on the farm had been "what it still is— roaming the woods."[217]

The city proper was small when she arrived, but growing at an alarming rate. Vast stretches of fields and woodland circled the developed area. West of Humboldt Avenue lay wetlands and woods all the way to Lake Minnetonka. Tamarack bogs near lakes Calhoun and Harriet and a marsh adjacent to Lake of the Isles were fine places for "botanizing." The land below Minnehaha Falls was rich with wildflowers. Recalling those spots later, Eloise wrote:

In the early '80s Minneapolis was a place of enchantment—a veritable fairyland. Along the river banks grew in profusion trillium, bloodroot, wild phlox, anemones, Dutchman's breeches, and

hepatica; the meadows were glorious with Indian paint brush,
both red and yellow, with gentians, purple fringed orchids, and
royal clumps of blue violets. In the tamarack swamps of the
suburbs might be seen long vistas of our state flower, the showy
lady's-slipper, together with the wild calla, and pitcher plants
without number.[218]

A botany teacher at Minneapolis's Central and South high schools, Butler not only built and used an herbarium, she took students on hikes into the countryside to show them natural plant communities. Laboring long and hard during her thirty-three years in Minneapolis classrooms, she lobbied for microscopes and greenhouses and wrote to leading science teachers to discover the most effective teaching methods. But botanizing, not teaching, was her great love, and she spent most weekends and holidays collecting and identifying specimens of Minnesota flora. Increasingly, she came to lament the loss of wild places to developers:

The shy woodland plants are fast dying out on our river banks; the
tamarack swamps have been drained, and with the drying up of the
water have disappeared the wondrous orchids and the strange
insectivorous plants.[219]

What was needed, she felt, was land close to the city, accessible to students and the public, where native plants could be nurtured and observed. Butler wanted this place to be different from typical botanical gardens arranged in formal beds. Her garden was to be wild.[220]

Gathering support for her proposal, a natural botanical garden for the instruction of students and for the enjoyment of all lovers of nature, she secured the signatures of every high school principal in the city, University of Minnesota President Cyrus Northrup, and numerous members of the university's science faculty.[221] The Minneapolis Board of Park Commissioners granted the request on April 7, 1907; on April 27, Eloise and her fellow botany teachers opened the garden, a section of Glenwood Park (now Theodore Wirth Park) on the western edge of the city.

The garden site had been carefully selected. A spring-fed tamarack bog sheltered by high wooded hillsides, the area was captivating. "Among the notables," Butler said, "were sundew, pitcher plant, Linnaea, Turk's cap lily, the two species of fringed gentian, showy and yellow lady-slipper."[222] Over the next years, Butler and her botanizing friends added thousands of ferns, trees, shrubs, and wildflowers to this rich collection.

Her intention was to establish flora from all regions of Minnesota, so that "within a space of twenty acres may be seen in an hour what would be impossible to find in traversing the state for several days."[223] She also added plants from her New England childhood. Butler was not yet retired from teaching, but her volunteer work at the Wild Botanic Garden became her passion. For four years she collected and planted, made an inventory of existing species, kept a garden logbook, and narrated tours for visitors.

In 1911, at the written request of the Conservation Committee of the Minneapolis Woman's Club, the Minneapolis Board of Park Commissioners created the position of curator of the garden and appointed Butler to the post. She held the title until her death in 1933.

Though unable to secure optimal funding for the garden, Butler managed to develop an impressive native plant collection, even by today's standards. The area continues to delight and educate thousands of visitors each year.

The garden's four habitats—woodland, wetland, upland, and prairie—make for interesting viewing in any season. Visitors can still observe several rare species established during Butler's tenure, including snow trillium, golden-seal, Christmas fern, Minnesota dwarf trout lily, twinleaf, and shooting star.[224] Many wildflower sanctuaries now exist throughout the United States, but Eloise Butler's garden was unique for its time. It is the oldest public wildflower garden in the United States and important for the early attention it focused on saving Minnesota's wild places.

·—◆—·

Marsh marigolds in the Eloise Butler Wildflower Garden.

The climates of Berkshire, England, and Hitterdal, Minnesota, (just east of Fargo) are latitudes apart. Still, Richard Herring and his brother William were undeterred when trying to recreate the English botanical gardens they had visited as children. Over a period of several decades, the brothers designed and maintained in Hitterdal their Floral Park, a garden the size of a city block.

The two came to Lake Park in Becker County from Sutton-Courtney, Berkshire, England, and operated the W. H. R. Herring store, selling "dry goods, groceries, hats, caps, boots, shoes, notions, [etc.]" through 1903.[225] Apparently they were successful, and in 1905 they built a larger general store in Hitterdal, twenty miles northwest of Lake Park. Just when the brothers started their flower garden is unknown. The first mention of Floral Park appeared in a local paper on September 11, 1914. Both men maintained the garden, but Richard planned the designs.[226]

Richard's inspiration may have been England's botanic gardens, but his own designs owed as much to "Prairie Eclectic" as to English borders. Certainly, the plant life was varied and exemplary. There were large flower gardens with many unusual flowers, trees, and vines.[227] Oranges, grapefruit, and a strawberry guava grew there, along with a variety of annuals and perennials. At least one year Richard won prizes for his entries at the county fair:[228]

What made the park unique is that it not only consisted of beautiful floral arrangements, but castoff metal parts, glass insulators, and rock piles. Over the years Richard added mock structures—temples, a forest ranger's cabin, a miniature English country church, a Russian cathedral, and "many other charming replicas of famous churches and castles,"[229] using junk of all descriptions as building blocks. A discarded fire hydrant, for example, became an elegant castle turret. By the 1930s Floral Park was known as Castle Gardens because of the great array of castles within its borders.

Floral Park made Hitterdal famous. The garden ran about two hundred feet along the railroad track and proved so popular that it drew tourists from miles around. People would come by train, pay the ten cents entry fee, and then catch the next train back.[230] Richard, ever the "British-looking gardener," was on hand to give a guided tour, describing the significance of his various creations. He was especially fond of pointing to the graves of his beloved dogs,

Tanner I and Tanner II, while their descendants trailed at his heels.

The Northern Pacific Railroad capitalized on the garden's fame by publishing a pamphlet advertising the park. Local papers kept readers up-to-date on what was blooming and what new features were to be seen—a miniature reproduction of "the Argonne forest in the time of peace" with Mexican firebush for trees or an "American soldier standing on a pedestal in the center of the Meuse River."[231] A photographer from Fargo sold views of the Floral Park to the International News Service.

William died in 1926, but Richard lived until 1950, keeping up the garden all the while. After his death, the gardens were maintained by volunteers until 1977 when the property was sold to the town. The east side of Castle Gardens became the town park; the bulbs and annuals planted there by the Ulen-Hitterdal Community Club are a reminder of the Herrings' elaborate flower beds.

The Herrings' Floral Park in Hitterdal about 1917, as seen from a Northern Pacific train.

PUBLIC EFFORTS
PRIVATE BENEFITS

The Park Commission has also undertaken to improve little neglected strips of land. . . .
These little spaces have been improved with shrubs and flower beds and are choice little
spots that greet the eyes of the visitor and reflect credit to the civic pride of the city.

E. D. Philbrick, Virginia Superintendent of Parks, 1915.[232]

Shared lives give rise to shared beliefs; in the common life of twentieth-century Minnesota, the importance of gardens and gardening was widely taken for granted. Just as individuals like Anna Underwood and Eloise Butler understood the benefits of having green space, so, too, did businesses, schools, and hospitals champion parks and greenery. Gardens sprouted in the heart of Minneapolis and at railroad depots along the Great Northern and Northern Pacific lines.

Towns and cities boasted to outsiders of their parks and gardens. Winona proclaimed Levee Park its *pièce de résistance*. Minneapolis advertised itself as the "City of Parks and Homes" and later, the "City of Lakes and Gardens." St. Paul was said to be the "City of Flowers and Birds."[233] There is some truth in these claims, but city promoters surely realized that green space was good for business.

As the Minneapolis design firm Morell and Nichols stated in its plan for Stillwater:

Minnesota Historical Society

*It is a well-established fact that a city, besides its valuable sites for commercial and industrial purposes, can have no greater asset than a well-planned system of public parks. . . . Besides the great pleasure afforded the inhabitants of the city . . . the fame of such civic improvements spreads rapidly throughout the country. . . . It may also be mentioned that . . . such improvements also represent a well-paying investment."[234]

Some of the demand for increased park land came from changed working conditions. Shorter work weeks, larger incomes, earlier retirement, and longer vacations left people with more leisure time. Cities responded by establishing bathing beaches, picnic areas, and bridle paths. Mankato added

Washington Park and Willard Parkway. Virginia dedicated Olcott Park, a tract of forty acres.

·—◆—·

An early glass lantern slide captures the Lyndale Park lilac grove in spring. Inset: Theodore Wirth.

This civic brochure was prepared about 1912.

During the years Theodore Wirth was superintendent of parks (1906-1933), Minneapolis's park system grew from 1,500 to 5,350 acres. Several lakes and their adjoining lands (Hiawatha, Cedar, Diamond, and Glenwood among them) were acquired. The Grand Rounds of Parkways, the name given to the city's encircling network of parks, was nearly completed, bringing the length from thirty-one miles in 1906 to sixty-two in 1945.[235]

Wirth, and other park supervisors watched their areas expand to include not only unstructured recreation, but also organized sports, gardening, and group activities such as dramatics, singing,

and crafts. Much of the additional space was earmarked for ball fields and golf courses. Wirth encouraged these changes, requesting that "Keep Off the Grass" signs be removed and adding staff to supervise children at play. Still, natural beauty remained a major attraction. Minneapolis, guided by Wirth, managed to balance recreational needs with landscaped beauty.

The aesthetic aspect of parks had long been an ideal to the Minneapolis Park and Recreation Board. In 1883 landscape architect Horace W. Cleveland addressed the board with his "Suggestions for a System of Parks and Parkways for the City of Minneapolis." He argued for preservation of the rugged beauty of the Mississippi River basin, for broad park drives along the riverbanks, and for a tree-lined circuit of parkways.[236] Cleveland spoke earnestly of the unspoiled beauty still within the city's borders and strongly urged the commissioners not to

shrink from securing while you may such areas as will be adequate for the wants of such a [great] city. Do not be appalled at the thought of appropriating lands which now seem costly, simply because they are far out of proportion to your present wants. . . . Look forward for a century, to the time when the city has a population of a million, and think what will be their wants.[237]

Cleveland's pleas had the desired effect and the board worked to acquire important park property throughout the century. Minnehaha Park and Parkway and the east bank of the Mississippi River were added during the late 1880s.

Wirth thus inherited a healthy, growing park system. His role was to expand and refine its beauty, adding not only land but lilac groves, chrysanthemum shows, and gardens of several kinds. Indeed, wrote Wirth, when considering various aspects of his park jurisdiction, "I give horticulture the lead in the divisional assignments."[238]

Wirth's background in floriculture may well explain his preference. Born in 1863 in Winterthur, Switzerland, Wirth developed an interest in flowers through childhood visits to the florist across the street from his home. Following high school and a three-year horticultural apprenticeship, he studied engineering

and at age twenty began his career in the landscape department of the 1883 National Exhibition in Zurich. For the next five years he worked for a London florist, the Jardin des Plantes in Paris, and the city parks of Zurich.[239]

In 1888 Wirth emigrated to America and worked on private estates and as a foreman with the New York City Park Department. He must have established an excellent reputation, for in 1896 he was hired as Superintendent of Parks in Hartford, Connecticut. Ten years later Charles Loring, president of the Minneapolis Board of Park Commissioners, tried to lure him westward, offering the park superintendent position in a letter. When that failed, Loring wisely sent a train ticket so that Wirth could inspect Minneapolis firsthand.

Though he was impressed with the growing park system, Wirth left Minnesota, fully intending to return to his place in Connecticut. But as the train rolled across the country, he remembered the beauty of Minnesota's creeks and wooded hills and became excited about the possibilities of developing a new park system. Wirth moved to Minnesota in January 1906, after insisting on certain "perks." He wanted a large combination house and office like the one he'd left behind and the right to bring two employees from Connecticut, horticulturist Louis Boeglin and Christian Bossen as his assistant.[240]

One of Wirth's first steps as superintendent was to design and establish a public rose garden, a novel idea at the time. In fact, at his previous post in Hartford, Wirth had developed the first municipal rose garden in America.[241]

The garden served as a testing ground for hardy varieties and as a stimulus for home rose culture. Wirth explained, "Outdoor rose culture had not been much in vogue in this part of the country, as it was considered too difficult, too uncertain of results, and too laborious an undertaking in our northern climate."[242] The one and one-half acre garden contained about 4,000 plants, 250 varieties in all, arranged in rows and surrounded by wild and shrub roses. Trellises enclosed the garden and arches spanned the walks; climbing roses covered both.

The Lyndale Park Rose Garden in Minneapolis has been popular since it opened in the summer of 1908.

The Lyndale Park Rose Garden opened in the summer of 1908 to enthusiastic crowds and has remained a favorite spot ever since. Over the years, weddings, baptisms, and many special events have taken place within its gates. For his work in originating public rose gardens in the United States, Wirth was awarded a gold medal in 1938 by the American Rose Society.[243]

Wirth was aware of the needs of home gardeners. To exhibit plants that would thrive in Minnesota, he added in city spaces, besides the rose garden, a rock garden, perennial borders, an arboretum, and collections of evergreens, lilacs, and peonies. Wirth also designed the Armory Garden to help stimulate amateur gardeners. Begun in 1913 as a display for the convention of the Society of American Florists and Ornamental Horticulture, the garden demonstrated that "the climate is not so adverse to successful achievements in floriculture as some people are inclined to believe."[244]

Set on park land adjoining "The Parade" on Lyndale Avenue next to the old Armory, where the florists' convention was held, the series of formal beds showcased hundreds of bulbs, annuals, and perennials. The garden, said Wirth, "received the unstinted praise of all who saw it."[245] So popular was the spot that for decades the beds were retained and maintained by the park staff as demonstration gardens. Freeway construction eventually claimed some of the site, but since 1988 the Minneapolis Sculpture Garden has restored beauty to the area.

Landscaping was by no means a routine aspect of establishing a business. In fact, in 1904 when Minneapolis's Cream of Wheat Company built a large, enclosed Italian garden for its employees, the *Minneapolis Journal* remarked that the company had "sacrificed what some men would consider business ideas by devoting a part of their plot to a garden."[246] Laid out by Warren H. Manning, the nationally-known landscape designer, the garden included a succession of perennials such as peony, bleeding heart, and tiger lily along with annuals to brighten up the summer and fall. Columns were draped with bittersweet and clematis. Yet the idea of industrial landscaping was not entirely novel. The St. Paul landscape firm of Holm & Olson published booklets in 1911 and 1920 extolling the benefits of landscaped businesses, schools, and hospitals, and several prominent firms planted gardens and trees.

John S. Bradstreet's Japanese garden (right) at his shop and crafthouse on the corner of Seventh Street and Fourth Avenue South embellished the most elaborately landscaped business in Minneapolis. A leading interior decorator and furniture designer, Bradstreet operated an enormous enterprise that included galleries, shops, and a furniture factory employing about eighty craftsmen.[247]

A devotee of Japanese culture, Bradstreet traveled to the Orient every other year, bringing back splendid artifacts for his home and garden. During the early 1890s he toured some of the celebrated gardens of Japan. When remodeling the crafthouse, Bradstreet transformed the side yard into a modified *hira-niwa*, or flat garden, with large boulders, evergreens, and incidental Japanese screen fences.[248] The crafthouse garden, featured in promotional material about Minneapolis, served as a display for Bradstreet's landscaping business as well as a pleasant personal retreat. In addition, Bradstreet had a fine Japanese garden at his home and even dreamed of building a large-scale park with Japanese features around Lake of the Isles. Though he sent sketches and proposals to the park commissioners, the work never materialized.[249]

The crafthouse survived only a few years after Bradstreet's death in 1914 as a result of an automobile accident, but in its day the garden brought fame to its owner and attention to the city.

Railroad companies may seem to be unlikely horticulturists, but even they paid attention to landscaping. The Great Northern had an orderly system during the 1920s for beautifying the sites of important depots along the line.

In the small community of Elk, Washington, agent George Dishmaker upgraded his station to the point that it drew the attention of Great Northern officials. He was made superintendent of parks, with orders to carry out his program at locations all the way to St. Paul. Moving quickly, Dishmaker built a greenhouse at the Monroe station in Washington, where flowers were grown for the dining cars and for supplying stations from Washington to Minnesota. Petunias, cannas, geraniums, vinca vines, and other flowers were provided for their window boxes, flower beds, and hanging baskets. Mr. Dishmaker rode the line each season to oversee local efforts.[250]

To check out the competition, Northern Pacific sent several of its agents along the Great Northern line to look at Dishmaker's work. Thanks to a precise report from agent F. J. Elliott, we have detailed information about Great Northern's "parks," as the company termed its landscaped station grounds.

There were a variety of flowers in the beds, Elliott wrote, but "Cannas predominate as these flowers thrive under almost any condition, and . . . will produce . . . large spikes of beautiful

flowers of unusually bright colors. Some of the beds have a candy tuft border, which is a small white flower, others a stone border painted white."[251]

Hanging baskets of geraniums and vinca vines were placed to face the trains. Petunias prevailed in the flower boxes, because "no other flower produces a greater diversity of color or retains its freshness for so long."[252] In Minnesota, small replicas of Red River oxcarts held a prominent place in landscaping schemes.

According to Elliott's report, depots were landscaped at Monticello, Sauk Centre, Brainerd, Moorhead, Wayzata, Willmar, and Breckenridge. St. Cloud and Alexandria were Minnesota's showplaces, with fine lawns and shrubbery, numerous flower beds and window boxes, and the requisite oxcart. About Alexandria, Elliott commented: "The grounds are very attractive. At Monroe I was advised that they shipped a third of a carload of flowers to Alexandria and the agent wanted more."[253]

Elliott concluded, "I think this park system is working out very nicely. . . . You will note that they have spent more time and money at stations where the trains stop for a few minutes or terminals [which] will come under the eye of passengers."[254]

Not only were gardens recognized as valuable, but the act of gardening itself was thought to improve character. Contact with nature, physical exercise, and a sense of stewardship were seen as contributors to mental health and moral development. Public schools, mining companies, and hospitals for the mentally ill instituted gardening programs, involving thousands of Minnesotans. The tenth annual report for the St. Peter State Hospital stated:

There can be no doubt as to the value of a greenhouse in connection with a hospital. . . . We call it the convalescent ward for men because more than any one other means at our command it aids in bringing about the recovery of those among the recent cases who can be induced to work among the plants and flowers.[255]

Mining companies initiated gardening programs to upgrade residential living conditions, providing free seeds and garden space; employees gardened on company grounds or at home. Cash prizes were awarded for the most attractive yards and gardens, and the winners' names were posted in company bulletins.

Participation was widespread. In 1919 Oliver Iron Mining had 2,078 contestants and gave away $908.80 in prizes. The company estimated the value of employee crops that year at $80,801.95.[256] Companies discovered that gardens did more than provide food. As stated in a United States Steel pamphlet, "The man's standing in the community is raised; his own self-respect is promoted."[257] We can assume the woman's standing was raised as well.

Public schools had a mix of motives for promoting school gardening programs. During World War I children were encouraged to raise vegetables for their families so that commercially grown food could be available to soldiers. In addition, gardens kept young people "off the street" and helped incorporate newcomers and immigrants into the community. School officials, especially, worried about the ills of industrialized life. Dietrich Lange, principal of St. Paul's Humboldt High School, noted in 1910, "It is now recognized that modern city life offers little opportunity for boys and girls to observe things outside."[258]

•——◆——•

Minnesota Historical Society

Children harvesting radishes in a St. Paul school garden in 1915.

St. Paul and Minneapolis offered summer gardening programs near school grounds and at students' homes; small towns and rural areas, helped by the Minnesota State Horticultural Society and the Agricultural Extension Division of the University, sponsored school garden clubs. Teachers or team leaders taught basic gardening skills, monitored their students' work throughout the summer, and judged results at season's end.

In an era before summer camps and organized sports, the programs were immensely popular. In 1915 about twelve hundred St. Paul students were actively gardening. By 1916 the program had grown so large that it named Alfred G. Perkins as Director of School Gardening.[259] In 1920 more than eighteen thousand students were involved statewide.

The program's appeal was not limited to gardening; harvest festivals, garden conventions, picnics, and music were all part of the mix. Local recipients of gardening awards were sent to the Minnesota State Fair. Participants from outstate were brought to the Twin Cities for tours. No wonder young people got excited about gardening. Edwin Neeb of Winona, a state champion in 1920 explained:

I was allowed to represent the southern districts . . . at

the Horticultural Society's meeting in December. . . .

We took trips around the cities. It was my first trip to

the Twin Cities and I shall never forget those trips. So when the

spring of 1920 came, I was ready for my third year's work.[260]

It is possible to imagine many of the era's gardens in present-day Minnesota. However, one enormous garden, renowned in its day, would intrigue modern Minnesotans. In 1911, under the direction of Professor Edwin L. Newcomb, the senior class in the University of Minnesota College of Pharmacy planted a one-acre medicinal plant garden. Sited where Northrup Auditorium now stands, the geometric plots were a "thing of beauty and utility,"[261] according to contemporary reports. Over eighty beds of varying sizes were separated by paths, surrounded by a buckthorn hedge, and interspersed with trees. The students grew belladonna, digitalis, datura, matricaria, valerian, and herbs too numerous to

mention. "It would be difficult to overestimate the value of this fieldwork in pharmacognosy [the branch of pharmacy dealing with crude or natural drugs]," reported *Northwestern Druggist* magazine. "The student, by handling these plants and by his close work with them, has at once the correct idea impressed upon his mind of the character of such drugs as Digitalis, Belladonna folia, etc."[262]

The university's garden (pictured above in 1910) drew attention for two reasons: the great variety of medicinal plants under cultivation and the small number of similar gardens in the United States. Cannibis (marijuana) was one of the specimens which aroused much interest, and visitors could frequently be observed studying the plants. In response, the College of Pharmacy in 1937 issued an official policy "of not giving out any information on identification, location, etc. of Marihuana to irresponsible persons."[263]

By 1935 thousands of plants were growing at the two-and-one-half-acre site on University Avenue. After World War II, an altered pharmacology field, in which chemicals could be synthesized rather than derived from plants, meant a diminished role for the garden and it was eventually eliminated. A greenhouse on River Road, maintained by the Department of Pharmacognosy, is all that remains of this once important teaching tool.

Lynn Steiner

HOME GROUND

1930 - 1948

—◆—

*The archway and terrace in the
Hernke garden at 1994 Summit, St. Paul,
have been preserved since the 1930s.*

OUTDOOR
LIVING ROOMS

"She's out in the garden," is the response given to any inquiry concerning members of the
Lake Minnetonka Garden Club these days. With trowels in hand the members . . . are
welcoming each hour of sunshine and . . . coaxing the spring plants into bloom. The
flower show of the Lake Minnetonka Garden Club . . . is the reason.

Minneapolis Journal, May, 1936.[264]

After the free-wheeling early twentieth century, the years following the financial crash of 1929 were times of reappraisal. Certainly, the century's first three decades had not been without their troubles. The First World War was a blow to the idea of uninterrupted progress, but the shocking days of October, 1929, put an end to what remained of America's youthful optimism.

As Minnesotans worked to come to terms with the economics of scarcity, they focused on home and family. Travel was curtailed. Wages were low. Hard times forced people to keep their pleasures close to home. What could be closer to home than a garden?

Gardening had long been a state tradition. Minnesota's Italian population was known for its lush gardens, both vegetables and grape arbors. Polish families established houses reminiscent of the home country, with flower gardens in front, orchards and vegetables in the rear.[265] German settlers took pride in neat yards, colorful flowers, and well-tended food crops. Farm families grew produce and flowers in the yard. Enthusiastic amateurs, like John W. G. Dunn of Lincoln Avenue in St. Paul, produced remarkable variety on city lots—raspberries and apples and bushels of vegetables along with zinnias and peonies (being admired by Dunn's son Jack, right). Some, like Dunn, kept meticulous records of late snows and early frosts, crop yields, and work accomplished, giving an accurate picture of home gardening in the first decades of the century.[266]

During the Depression, gardening became even more widespread. Garden club member Mrs. M. L. Richardson of Comfrey, Minnesota, noted:

In a garden we can get away from the every-day worries
and cares. . . . Many men and women, who did not take any interest
in working with plants a few years ago, have become enthusiastic
garden fans, and caring for the home garden has become America's
No. 1 hobby.[267]

THREE FOREMOST
RADISHES
- 1 Packet Each
F.S.&N.Co's Early Red Robin
F.S.&N.Co's Sparkler White Tip
F.S.&N.Co's White Icicle
All for 25¢ Postpaid

FARMER SEED
AND
NURSERY CO.

1928   FARIBAULT, MINN.

Garden clubs flourished; garden tours continued unabated. Members of 4-H clubs adopted home beautification projects. Not even prolonged drought and fierce heat managed to discourage gardeners entirely. In its coverage of the 1930 Fall Flower Show, the Moorhead newspaper reported:

Beauty of the exhibits is described as a sharp contrast to expectations of below par flowers following the unusual drouth conditions of summer, and is scored as a demonstration of skill by the amateur gardeners.[268]

Newspapers were full of garden advice: "How to bring fragrance into the garden," "Strawberries easy to grow on home lot," and "Hardy annuals thrive in poorest soil." One can look in vain for any mention of the Depression engulfing the country.

Rather, gardeners were advised that "It's not a Home Until It's Planted" and encouraged to think of the back yard as an "outdoor living room," where "children are safe from the dangers of the street" and "men can relax and find recreation in the evenings." The garden, then, became a respite from the difficult world, a place where the whole family could find "seclusion from the public," and "recreation in healthful surroundings."[269]

Pictures of the time reveal cozy, inviting spaces in which picket fences and shrubbery enclose the yard and provide a background for flowering plants—perennials, annuals, and bulbs. The old stalwarts, including iris, daylilies, hollyhocks, peonies, phlox, roses, and lilacs, grow in colorful masses along the fence. Sweet peas and clematis clamor across the trellis. Bird baths, small ponds, and rock gardens share space with benches and lawn furniture, beckoning the family to sit for a time. The effect is one of comfort and serenity, with not a hint of the problems outside.

Perhaps, in the 1930s, that was the point. Families might not be able to turn the tide of the economy, but they could create a

· — ◆ — ·

Nurseries and seed houses recognized the large number of middle-class women gardeners. This catalogue was distributed by Farmer Seed and Nursery Company in 1928.

comfortable sanctuary at home.

The general enthusiasm for gardening created some interesting yards. Most front lawns followed the conventions of the time: smooth grass and foundation plantings of evergreens or flowering shrubs. Behind the house, gardeners created a more personal space. To eyes accustomed to contemporary, slicked-down suburban lawns, the back yard of the thirties might appear crowded. Besides flowers and a vegetable plot, gardens contained structures. Arbors and archways were popular, but windmills, wishing wells, and miniature railroads were also in vogue. "One familiar device," reported the *Minneapolis Journal*, "[is] the sweet pea trellis which [furnishes] an attractive background of flowers with small sacrifice of space."[270] Various kinds of rock and stone were used for retaining walls and sitting areas.

Back-yard ponds were in every neighborhood. People of means often incorporated elegant, rectangular lily ponds into terraces and lawns. Homeowners of modest incomes built small ovals banked with limestone and filled with lilies. Newspaper and magazine articles described the construction process and how to add waterfalls and fountains. Nursery catalogues offered water plants. The craze was not limited to Minnesotans. By 1935 so many yards across the United States had potentially mosquito-breeding ponds that public health officials warned of a possible outbreak of malaria.[271]

Perhaps the most common garden feature of the thirties was the rockery. Ranging in size from the one and one-half-acre site at Lake Harriet to tiny back-yard plots, rock gardens flourished in every corner of the state, and many became quite elaborate over time. The rock garden of the Garfield Rustads in Moorhead exemplified this trend.

. . . the back yard . . . had been transformed into a place of magic with lighted water pools adorned with lilies; a rustic bridge; an artistically fashioned rock pile with a waterfall and profusion of flowers; a replica of a Dutch mill, fountains, terraces and flower beds which present a riot of color.[272]

Rock gardens evolved from season to season, as gardeners found unusual stones or added structures. John Christensen, a retired farmer near Albert Lea, expanded his garden with rocks brought by friends from "every state in the Union . . . the Black Hills

Mrs. John S. Dalrymple's lush rock garden at Crystal Bay, Lake Minnetonka, was featured on garden tours.

·——◆——·

and everywhere."[273] He constructed stone bird houses, a sun dial, a stone bridge, and castles built to scale. Like Christensen, who worked to recreate the image he had of his Danish homeland, gardeners often constructed replicas of familiar landscapes, such as farms, log cabins, and mountains of Europe.

Not all rock-garden devotees were men. Alpha Chi Omega sorority at the University of Minnesota built a rockery that was featured in the *Minneapolis Journal*.[274] Amateur gardener Ragna "Rags" Lindgren, eighty years old in 1994, remembered her St. Paul garden, started in 1939 with rocks collected on her honeymoon. "There was no plan to it. It was just a mound under the mountain ash tree. We added to it whenever we'd find some pretty stones." Other memorable rocks were from a friend in Illinois, "the kind they made buttons out of," and some lovely grooved stones from the banks of the Mississippi River. The Lindgrens planted their garden with hens-and-chicks, Johnny-jump-ups, and other small plants. "Rock gardens were quite the thing," she recalled.[275]

Gardeners could choose plants grown locally. Ferndale Nursery in Askov specialized in hardy ferns, wild and rock garden plants, offering nearly three hundred varieties, achillea to violas, in its mail-order catalogue. Included in each mailing were directions for constructing and planting the garden. "The spirit of the rockery is essentially natural," the nursery advised.[276] Other firms catered to the rock garden market. Holm & Olson in St. Paul offered a "Rock Plant Collection" and distributed a booklet, *The Home Yard Rock Garden*.

Large rock gardens attracted visitors and publicity. Ak Sar Ben (Nebraska spelled backwards) Gardens on Tame Fish Lake lured thousands of tourists each summer.[277] The Vogt brothers, Arnold the gardener and Hugo the builder, started Ak Sar Ben in 1918 as part of a summer's idyll at the lake, and by 1939 they had added castles, fountains, pools, and thousands of plants. So many visitors arrived (forty thousand that season) that the Vogts were forced to charge ten cents admission to cover maintenance and minor damages. Norma Talmadge and Will Rogers were among the celebrities to sign the guest register.

Most back-yard rock gardens were more modest affairs, emphasizing the plants rather than stones. Their appeal, explained Ludvig Mosbaek, proprietor of Ferndale Nurseries, was twofold: A rock garden afforded a "delightful diversion from a formal type of garden" and, perhaps, most importantly, "expert hands are not needed."[278]

To satisfy a curious public, newspapers and magazines covered gardening extensively. Every Sunday the *Minneapolis Journal* carried "Home, Garden, Lawn, and Flowers," which later became "Timely Garden Tips." The society page reported garden club activities and tours. Large flower exhibitions were worthy of the front page.

By the late 1930s newspapers featured regular garden columnists. George Luxton, who had achieved fame as a photo-journalist, enjoyed a thirty-year run in the *Minneapolis Journal*. At the *Mankato Free Press*, Walt Scherer, known as the "Enthusiastic Gardener," wrote a column from 1938 until 1965. Though hampered by poor health, he wrote occasionally until his death in 1970. Daisy Abbott, a Crocus Hill resident and British native, provided gentle advice to readers of the *St. Paul Pioneer Press Dispatch*.

All three were amateur gardeners, drawn to writing because of their great love for gardening and because others asked their advice so frequently. Abbott started her column "Our Minnesota Garden, a corner where the amateur can receive instruction," because she was so "besieged with telephone calls about gardening and flowers."[279]

All three writers were in demand as flower show judges and as speakers at garden clubs. Luxton wrote *Flower Growing in the North*, for years the standard source in Minnesota for information on perennials. Abbott wrote *The Northern Garden, Week by Week* in 1938 and *The Indoor Gardener* in 1939. Scherer published *The Enthusiastic Gardener* in book form after his readers requested more than his newspaper column.

Nothing demonstrates Minnesotans' high level of interest in gardening more clearly than the rate at which they organized garden clubs. Almost every town had one club, and larger towns had several. By their hard work and influence, the groups helped to beautify the communities in which they lived.

The earliest, of course, was the Ladies Floral Society in Austin, begun in 1869. One of the oldest amateur groups was the Minnesota Rose Society, founded in 1904 in Minneapolis. It broadened its intent and in 1911 became the Minnesota Garden Flower Society. Most Minnesota garden clubs, however, were organized in the years between the world wars. By 1950 there were thousands of men and women in 185 clubs affiliated with the Minnesota State Horticultural Society and countless others who were in unaffiliated groups. Some, like

A woman with her prize-winning
gladiola at the Minnesota State Fair in 1926.

the Garden Club of Ramsey County, had memberships of fifty to seven hundred and scheduled elaborate programs.

During its first year of existence (1934), the twenty-eight-member Monticello Garden Club had a full agenda. In addition to meeting every two weeks, except during July and August, the club sponsored two garden picnics, replanted the band park, held a Garden Mart and flower show, and organized a city-wide competition for home gardeners, vegetable gardeners, and the landscapers of businesses and public buildings.[280]

That same year the Garden Club of Ramsey County counted three hundred members and averaged one hundred per session. The group maintained booths at the Ramsey County and Minnesota State Fairs, and it organized garden tours. Members also sponsored a flower show and a Garden and Lawn Contest which drew 150 entrants and much media coverage.[281]

By its tenth year (1937), the Duluth Garden Flower Society was the umbrella organization for twenty-three neighborhood groups. Civic work included "tree plantings, care of tennis courts, planting around many public buildings . . . care of a beautiful rock garden . . . and care of a public rose garden."[282] Members sent plants, gifts and food to orphanages and nursing homes, the Red Cross, and the Salvation Army. They staged flower shows that were "unusually successful considering the dry summer."[283]

In 1941 the Minnesota Garden Flower Society had a record high of 670 members from throughout the Twin Cities. Its 1936 budget ($996.95) included disbursements for the Audubon Society, a 4-H scholarship, seed distribution, and flowers for local hospitals.[284] Smaller clubs averaged twenty-five members, met in each other's homes, and produced their own programs.

In one long-standing effort to "Make Minnesota Blossom," the Minnesota Garden Flower Society furnished blooms and greenery to hospitalized veterans for over fifty years. The project was started in 1917 when the first World War I veterans arrived at Fort Snelling. Initially, members gathered bouquets from their yards and delivered them weekly. One newspaper appeal in 1922 reported that the soldiers particularly liked "the kind of flowers their mothers used to raise back home,"[285] including roses, lilies, sweet peas, corn flowers, snapdragons, cosmos, baby's breath, and pansies.

Whatever else they might schedule, clubs held flower shows and garden tours every year. During spring and summer, members opened their gardens to each other for what was then called the "pilgrimage." The Minnesota Garden Flower Society published a list of garden tours beginning in mid-May and continuing until late September. Over the course of the season, participants could travel from Lake Minnetonka, through Minneapolis and St. Paul, to White Bear Lake, and back to Lake Minnetonka. According to advance publicity, gardeners might expect to see numerous specialty gardens along the way—four thousand Dutch tulips at one Minneapolis home, five hundred varieties of flowers at another, a wildflower display in White Bear Lake, and an English garden in Lake Minnetonka.[286]

Visitors joining the 1946 Lake Minnetonka Garden Tour had a choice of twenty stops, including the architectural English garden of Mrs. John S. Pillsbury, a beautiful and unique rock garden kept by Mrs. George N. Dayton, or a circular garden of annuals and perennials belonging to Mrs. Franklin M. Crosby. Participants were advised to "Save yourself and the garden by wearing low heels."[287]

Garden clubs enthusiastically embraced flower shows. The Benson club, for example, held its first flower show in a vacant building in 1938; there were 33 entries, followed by 135 the next year. By 1940 there were 161 entries and one thousand visitors.[288] Competition was usually stiff at these events, with strict rules governing the proceedings and prizes for the winners. An exhibition might be organized around a particular flower; peony shows were thirties' favorites. Equally popular were contests in flower arranging. In its 1936 spring show the Lake Minnetonka Garden Club offered prizes in seven classes—porch arrangements, outdoor tables, picnic baskets, bottle plans, specimen blooms, window boxes, and flower arrangements. Successful contestants were encouraged to enter larger competitions, such as county fairs or the Minnesota State Fair.

When the Garden Section of the Minneapolis Woman's Club held its 1935 flower show, the event was a "gala occasion," according to the *Minnesota Horticulturist*. There were flower arrangements of "many beautiful and original effects, in vases, dish gardens, submerged bouquets, miniature rock gardens, bottle gardens, and the popular . . . soup tureens." The show was unusual because of the "utter absence of any premiums [or] judges, just the unqualified appreciation of all the beauty shown."[289]

Today, garden clubs continue to be robust forces in Minnesota, tackling city beautification projects, sponsoring tours of private and public gardens, and encouraging individual efforts. Part of their durability lies in the fact that members become friends. "There is wonderful companionship in working with people interested in the same things you are," said Anne Koempel, past president and long-time member of both the Garden Club of Ramsey County and the Minnesota Garden Flower Society.[290] But the Benson Garden Club in 1935 may have hit on an equally important factor. Its policy from the beginning has been "no gossip and no political or religious arguments, and everyone [needs to help] as much as possible."[291]

•———◆———•

Peony shows were the forerunner of more general flower shows. This one was held at the First National Bank in St. Paul in 1921.

THE HOME FRONT

Things look black for many of us just now. Our boys are gone to fight, and the work

piles up until it seems as though there isn't any use trying to do the impossible. . . .

Why not have a symbol of Hope in our own yards? I'm going to plant a

"Hope Tree" and when the going is tough I'll water the tree or

dig around it a bit and think of better times.

R. E. Hodgson, Superintendent, Southeast Experiment Station, Waseca, 1942.[292]

Mention the thirties and forties and strong images come to mind—the Depression, unemployment, the New Deal, World War II. Beautiful gardens seem an unlikely part of the mix, yet the era produced some lovely creations.

Intimate yards were the hallmark of these two decades, but many large estate gardens continued to thrive. Families whose fortunes were unharmed by the crash of 1929 added to, reworked, and maintained their grounds through the thirties. Glensheen and Mayowood were in their prime. Edmund Phelps, Minnesota-born and Harvard-trained landscape architect, continued to serve a small but loyal set of clients in the western suburbs of Minneapolis.

While sometimes forced to downscale maintenance, businesses worked hard to keep up appearances. Certain public institutions benefited from federal assistance that came with Franklin Roosevelt's New Deal legislation. Indeed, the government's presence had an effect on the landscape not seen previously. New Deal programs, especially those of the Works Progress Administration and the Civilian Conservation Corps, provided landscaping for public buildings and the expansion and improvement of state and city parks.

In parks around the state, WPA and CCC crews built greenhouses, retaining walls, and foot bridges. They cleared roadways and laid out nature trails. At St. Paul's Como Park, workers constructed stone pillars at its entrance, many new buildings, and a sunken garden.[293] Minnesota's state parks, so familiar now, took shape using CCC labor and funds, under the direction of architects and landscape designers hired by the National Park Service.

One of many cities to feel the helpful hand of the WPA was St. Cloud. Its park superintendent in the 1930s, Joseph P. Munsinger, was an efficient manager

In 1930 Minneapolis business people contributed funds to beautify the city with hanging baskets of flowers.

and "preeminently a flower grower."[294] When Munsinger was hired in 1928, Central Park (later called Barden) was about the only park that had been developed. At his death in 1946 he left St. Cloud with a comprehensive program of parks and recreation centers.[295]

When the WPA began its operations in St. Cloud in the late 1930s, Munsinger was able to move ahead more efficiently with his plans, adding a pool, rock garden, and arching stone bridge in the Williams Garden section of Eastman Park.[297] Planted with an abundance of flowers, the site received honorable mention in a nationwide contest for park beautification.

D.R. Martin

At Riverside Park on the east end of the Tenth Street bridge, WPA workers built a large rock garden and two lily pools, each with fountains. Stone walkways wound past beds of roses, tulips, peonies, lilies, phlox, and seventy-five varieties of irises. All were labeled so the public might note plants of interest for their home gardens.[298] Evergreens and shade trees dotted the lawns. In typical WPA fashion, pathways, ponds, and the rock garden were made of stones gathered from within a fifteen-mile area of town.

In 1938, in honor of the superintendent's intense involvement, the park was named Munsinger Gardens. "The tract, blazing with flowers and patterned by shrubbery, trees, stone walks, and cobblestone wells, [attracted] visitors

Munsinger was passionate about St. Cloud's parks. To increase his supply of flowers he traded varieties with the manager of the nearby Veterans Administration hospital greenhouse. When vandals destroyed many flowers in 1935, Munsinger was "not calm and collected when he described the situation,"[296] according to the local newspaper. The flowers were there to "look nice" for the benefit of all, he reminded citizens.

•—◆—•

The Munsinger gardens in St. Cloud, constructed with WPA crews, are as spectacular today as they were in the 1930s.

from many states."[299] Thanks to the work of the WPA, said a 1939 editorial, St. Cloud's "parks have been improved so that they are the pride of the city."[300]

Most landscapes from the thirties can be seen only in photographs; Munsinger Gardens is an exception. It continues to thrive and grow, nurtured over the decades by park crews. The pools and fountains are in fine shape; the rock garden and perennial beds are lush. The characteristic 1930s stonework is still intact.

In recent years, a new benefactor has come forward. Local businessman and park neighbor Bill Clemens donated an adjacent lot, then offered to foot the bills for a new rose garden to honor his wife Virginia. Later he provided a one million-dollar trust fund to make certain the garden will always be well tended.[301] Park staff have been able to enlarge the beds and walkways, blending the original site and new plantings and making Munsinger Gardens a gem among Minnesota's public gardens.

The Minnesota State Fairgrounds and its buildings were built in the 1930s largely by the WPA and its predecessor, the Economic Recovery Administration, in part because WPA District Engineer Kindy C. Wright was a great fan of the fair. The swine barns, sheep and poultry building, streets and sidewalks, and underground utilities—much that makes the fair unusually well-appointed—were built with WPA labor. The lavish gardens, though, were the work of Bill Vasatka, head of the greenhouse, and his crew.

In 1909 when Vasatka was hired, the fair already had a long tradition of elaborate floral displays. But Vasatka and C. N. Cosgrove, state fair secretary, were determined to make the grounds one of the most beautiful in the country. Their ambitious program included formal gardens, stately stands of canna lilies, shrubbery, and lines of shade trees. Most impressive was the sunken garden on the grandstand approach with its foliage borders and geometric pattern of square and circular beds. Over the years Vasatka added more features. The Floral Liberty Bell, accurate down to the crack in its side (simulated with pale green sedum), was started in 1921. Each summer the large wire-mesh bell, coated with a special blend of black earth and compost, was filled with fifteen thousand individual plants.[302]

In 1934, to celebrate the fair's Diamond Jubilee, the grounds were given a $120,000 facelift, which included new gardens and floral designs. At the streetcar entrance on Como, then the main gateway to the fair, grounds workers built a park with a sunken pool and illuminated fountain.

Vasatka's masterpiece that summer was the Gates Ajar planting, similar to a display of the same name at nearby Como Park. The idea may have originated with Fred Nussbaumer, St. Paul's first park superintendent; the image was a familiar one in parks of Germany, Nussbaumer's homeland.[303] The massive floral steps and gates symbolized the gates flung wide to heaven. Symbolism or no, visitors could appreciate the stunning display—wide steps leading to large, open gates, emblazoned with moon and star motif—all constructed with twenty-five thousand plants. According to fair historian Karal Ann Marling, visitors have taken more photographs of the Gates Ajar than any other feature at the fair.[304]

Gates Ajar, the Liberty Bell, and many of the hundred other beds and gardens around the grounds have endured. Greenhouse supervisors and crews are a loyal bunch—only five men have served as greenhouse superintendent since Vasatka began in 1909. Indeed, many garden techniques are the same as those used by Vasatka.[305] Workers continue to grow thousands of plants in the greenhouse each season (twelve thousand cannas alone), plant beds of geraniums, marigolds, and petunias, and fill the two vintage rock gardens, preserving, in the process, a part of the landscape as Vasatka envisioned it.

Public gardens during the thirties and forties were usually sponsored by a number of people. Little Bit O' Heaven in Alexandria was the work of a single benefactor: local son and businessman-made-good Phillip Noonan.[306] Noonan and his brother built their creamery business into one of the largest enterprises of its kind in the United States. Active on the park board and interested in making Alexandria a better and more beautiful city, Noonan could always be counted on for a generous contribution when City Park needed an attractive entryway or new tennis courts.

Noonan and his wife were great gardeners; Mollie gave away bushels of produce and gallons of canned sauerkraut. In 1929 they decided to convert their vegetable plot to a large formal garden that would be open to the public. Their motivation remains unclear, wrote Luverne Heimer, Noonan's secretary. "[It could have been] a lingering memory of the flaunting colors of California gardens, admired at winter vacation time . . . or a desire to do a little private prizeless competition in the zinnia contest that the Park Board was at that time sponsoring."[307]

Begun in the fall of 1929 and completed the following spring, Little Bit O' Heaven's layout (p. 98) was much like that of early

estate gardens. Visitors entered a tall latticed gate spanned by clipped hedges. Formal walks, punctuated by urns, led past parterres of iris, lilies, and gladiola, in addition to small trees and shrubs. In the distance, an elegant lily pool and massive pergola captured the eye. Trellised enclosures and flowering vines formed the border.

Two years later Noonan added an adjacent piece of property for a rock garden. Construction lasted two months and employed up to twenty-six men daily, a point of gratitude in a town gripped by the Depression. As Heimer described it,

A canvas tent fifty feet long, fourteen feet wide, and seven feet high, which was heated by stoves, made it possible for masons to construct the stone walls during the winter and early spring months. The limestone used in the walls of the rock garden and in the wishing well and brook linings was taken from the old Pillsbury "B" Mill in Minneapolis, which was erected in 1866 by Taylor Brothers and purchased in 1870 by C. A. Pillsbury. That was the second flour mill built in Minneapolis. More than 700,000 pounds of this limestone were used. The old moss-covered rocks in the garden came from the St. Croix Valley. Water [flowed] over the artificial falls at the rate of 35 gallons a minute.[308]

The two gardens, known collectively as "Little Bit O' Heaven," made Alexandria famous. In 1942 the town newspaper, *The Park Region Echo*, reported that "Each year thousands of tourists from all over the nation and Canada walk leisurely through this colorful flowerland."[309]

After Phil Noonan's death in 1945, his wife Mollie and her gardener tended the site for nine more seasons. In 1954 Mollie closed the gates twenty-five years after her husband had opened them. The land was later sold for homes, and the garden plants and ornaments dispersed. Only the tall birdhouse and a portion of the stone wall marking the rock garden remain as reminders of the quiet beauty that attracted so many.

Flowers in great masses, whether planted in enormous beds or gathered for shows, were characteristic of the period. Events like the 1930 National Flower and Garden Show in Minneapolis drew huge crowds; over sixty thousand people bought tickets before the show opened. "These national flower shows have the largest attendance of any shows staged anywhere in the country,"[310] said the *Minneapolis Tribune*. The event was held at the Municipal Auditorium under the auspices of the Society of American Florists and Ornamental Horticulturists and sponsored by the Minnesota State Florist Association.

For the show, florists and amateurs assembled the largest and most ambitious display of its kind in the Northwest: "rose gardens, tulip gardens, several rock gardens, complete from their running creeks to puffy toadstool . . . blossoming trees of all kinds [the] aristocrats of flowerland, the orchids [and] a mass of high palms. . . . The air of the auditorium [was] heavy with the fragrance of those thousands of plants."[311] Small wonder that trains ran special excursion routes to Minneapolis from towns around the state and school children came by the busload.

Other forms of floral massing were giant carpet-bedding schemes, including stars within circles, town seals, and patriotic symbols. St. John's University in Collegeville, as part of its very active horticulture program, for decades set aside a central plot for floral designs. At Olcott Park in Virginia, Gunnar Peterson created intricate designs incorporating numbers, words, and symbols. Peterson, who trained in Sweden and Germany and once worked for the King of Sweden, was Virginia's floral specialist for over thirty years.[312]

The state fair's Vasatka was a master at carpet-bed displays. During World War II his decorative plantings featured spectacular patriotic themes, and his 1942 design was perhaps the most memorable. On a sloping plot across from the grandstand, Vasatka installed a "living flag" containing more than twenty-one thousand plants in red, white, and blue. Measuring fifty-one by eighty-two feet, the flag ("believed to be the largest of its kind") contained 4,800 bleached hen-and-chicks plants for stars, silver maples for white stripes, and thousands of aeschynanthus (lipstick plant) for the red stripes. In a special ceremony on Navy Day, sailors stood at attention among the "stars," on rocks painted blue.[313]

Vasatka's "living flag" and other plots of patriotic design around the state were just one manifestation of the gardening frenzy that swept the United States during the war years. World War II was an all-out conflict that compelled every American to contribute. Young adults joined the armed services; folks at home saved scrap, used ration cards—and gardened.[314]

The summer of 1942 saw a heightened interest in home gardening, though not until 1943 was there a concerted effort to increase food production. American farmers were trying to feed Americans and keep half of Europe from starving. The military needed the gasoline and aluminum used by food producers. Victory gardens were viewed as wise investments because they used spare-time labor and idle lands. Those left at home were advised: "Food will win the war," "Plant a Victory garden or tighten your belt," and, in a slogan sure to appeal to kids, "Food fights the war."[315] Private gardens had become public policy.

The term Victory Garden had been coined at the end of World War I to encourage Americans to continue their allotment gardening. The Civilian Defense Council was the official government body promoting home gardening. In addition, the notion of Victory Gardening took on a life of its own, becoming both a family and community effort. Women, children, and the aged—all those left behind—successfully raised vegetables and fruit, a positive effort in the midst of uncertainty and sacrifice.

Help came from all sides. The Agricultural Extension Service at the University of Minnesota sponsored a regional Victory Gardening Conference. Governor Edward J. Thye and national and state agriculture leaders addressed the crowd on nutrition and problems of the home gardener. Companies like International Harvester issued posters and booklets on vegetable and fruit production. The *Minnesota Horticulturist* devoted several issues to home gardening.

During the growing season, it was difficult to open any newspaper without seeing one or two articles about the Victory Garden. *Minneapolis Tribune* columnist Cedric Adams discussed the topic and society writer Agnes Taafe wrote at length about who gardened where, produced how much, and canned what quantity—an interesting diversion from information about travel and weddings.[316] Gardeners' contributions to the war effort were underscored with the use of martial terms—"destroy," "invade," "fight," and "fifth column"—to describe plant-growing and weed-control techniques.

Railroads and other industries made their properties available to gardeners. Northern Pacific and the Great Northern railways allowed employees to plant on sections of station grounds and land along rights-of-way.[317] Twin City Rapid Transit Company provided land and prizes for its workers. Numerous other firms, including Swift and Company, American Hoist and Derrick, Minnesota Power and Light, and Northwest Airlines, established incentive plans for those who planted Victory gardens.

Minnesotans responded with zeal. In 1943, eleven hundred Duluth school children agreed to participate. The Twin Cities had 130,000 gardeners. In 1944 an estimated forty percent of all fresh vegetables on Minnesota tables was grown in Victory Gardens.[318] Nationally, twenty million gardeners joined the effort.

For some would-be gardeners, access to land was a problem. To meet that need, schools, parks, and vacant lots were plowed for community gardens. Duluth opened up six public locations—44 acres, 880 individual lots. For a small fee, participants were given a thirty-three by sixty-six-foot plot that had been plowed, harrowed, and fertilized. Supervisors were stationed at each site to advise and aid the inexperienced and the careless.[319]

Brochures and news articles informed gardeners of possible problems. One flyer in Duluth warned ominously that "potato and tomato blight has already appeared in the city, also cabbage, cauliflower and other vegetable bugs which not taken care of will be detrimental to good garden crops."[320] Food gardening had become a duty.

Efforts peaked in 1943 and 1944 when Allied forces were stretched to the limit to contain the Axis powers. By the winter of 1944, with the end in sight, officials like Frances Howe Satterlee of the Minneapolis Defense Council began to wonder about the role for gardeners in the summer of 1945 and beyond. Certain groups spoke of food surpluses, said Satterlee, and suggested that gardening shift away from food production. But Mrs. Satterlee and other experts were reluctant to give up gardening altogether. The benefits had been obvious, she noted. In addition to "keeping children occupied and off the streets" (apparently a perennial concern), the "gardening program [has] been productive of much good feeling. A wonderful community spirit has resulted because of friendly backfence hobnobbing; [so] it would seem . . . to be dangerous, just with one swish, to say we will no longer have a gardening program."[321]

Inevitably, as the need for food production diminished, Minnesotans' enthusiasm for vegetable growing took a back seat to ornamental gardening and creating the perfect lawn. But the community spirit, the organizational skills, and the ties made with governmental agencies were not lost, ready to be reactivated in the community gardening movement of later decades.

• — ◆ — •

Posters like this one urged those left at home—women, children, and the elderly—to grow food for victory.

T H E

G O O D   L I F E

1947 - 1970

·——◆——·

Linwood School kindergarten students tour the
Bernard H. Ridder garden on Lincoln Avenue in St. Paul
with their teacher Miss Patricia Shea in 1956.

L A W N S & R O S E S

A good lawn is the most important single feature of any home landscape.

Leon Snyder, *Minnesota Horticulturist*, 1953.[322]

*The lawn should be a broad, uninterrupted expanse of grass, for it
is the canvas on which we create our landscape picture.*

C. Gustav Hard, *Landscaping Your Home*, University of Minnesota Extension Bulletin, 1958.[323]

For thousands of young people returning to Minnesota from military duty, the post-war years were a time to get married, start a family, and buy a home. Having put their lives "on hold" during World War II, they were anxious to finish an education and establish roots. President Roosevelt's Servicemen's Readjustment Act of 1944, otherwise known as the GI Bill, made buying a house within the means of most. Slightly older couples, whose lives had also been sidetracked by the Depression and the war, found that the booming economy enabled them to finance new homes as well. The legacy of two decades of hardship and restriction was replaced with the greatest surge of home construction since the 1920s.[324]

Nationally, there was a fascination with California, where the living was easy. Magazines like *Better Homes and Gardens* praised the sunny openness of West Coast homes, with their emphasis on relaxation and livability.[325] Before World War II, California landscape architects used the same eclectic principles as the rest of the country. But after the war a small group of designers, led by Thomas Church and Garrett Eckbo, sought to create spaces that suited American plants, landscapes, and social patterns.[326] Their outdoor areas featured immense terraces and imaginative uses of concrete. The new designs had hard edges; plants were used mainly for accenting and softening. California ideas influenced large and small landscape design for decades.

In suburbs and new developments such as Bloomington and Falcon Heights, families moved into ranch-style homes with generous lots. The low-slung silhouette and simple style of the typical new house enabled Minnesotans to re-create a bit of California at home.

The new profile called for a scaled-down natural world. Vines, pergolas, and ponds looked out of place next to the house's square, spare lines. As University of Minnesota extension agent Gustav Hard explained, the "lawn, foundation plantings and permanent trees [were] the most important elements [in the front yard]."[327]

Trees, of course, were important because many new homes had been built on old farmland or lots stripped of vegetation for ease of construction. Foundation planting was essential—clipped yew, arborvitae, euonymous, juniper, and mugho pines accented vertical and horizontal lines of the home. "The purpose of a

foundation plantings and to give an attractive view for the ever-present picture window.[329] Concrete had many "structural advantages," Gustav Hard concluded in 1965, but tended "to present a cold hard surface." Also, he said, the "row-type treatment of front yards contributes to community monotony."[330] His suggestion: colorful flower beds and shrubbery to alleviate the sameness.

D.R. Martin

But if we are to judge by the ads and articles of the time, lawns, not shrubs or flowers, were the indispensable ingredient of the 1950s landscape. As such, they consumed the energies of homeowners across the state.

Lawns were not a new interest. Victorians valued a smooth swath of green to set off the house and gardens and to serve as a backdrop for croquet or tennis. Both Andrew Jackson Downing and

foundation planting," said Hard, "is to blend the house into the lawn."[328] Brochures and nursery catalogues demonstrated the proper placement and size of evergreens and shrubs. Flowers were relegated to perimeter beds around the edges of the lot or pots of annuals on the patio.

Not everyone applauded. The editor of *Home Garden* magazine called for a return to dooryard gardens to offset the austerity of

·—◆—·

Generous weed-free lawns typified the post-war years. A well-groomed carpet of grass outdoors was an extension of the plush, indoor wall-to-wall carpeting in newly built ranch-style homes.

Frederick Law Olmsted had lauded the aesthetic qualities of a broad expanse of turf. Edwin Budding's 1833 invention, the lawn mower, had become widely available by 1880, making the well-manicured lawn within easy reach of the average Victorian. Most early twentieth-century homes also sported a front yard of neatly trimmed grass, which gave privacy and separated the house from the street.

Not until the fifties, though, did a brilliant green, weed-free lawn become an obsession. Entire books were written detailing techniques for perfect turf. Sunset Books in California issued three editions of *Lawn and Ground Covers* between 1955 and 1964 because of the "quick pattern of change in the turfgrass business."[331] Starting in the 1940s, universities and seed and chemical companies began putting great amounts of time and money into research on home gardeners' problems and needs. Millions of new homes were creating a bigger demand for lawns and easier lawn maintenance. "The outcome was predictable: new grasses, new products, and new apparatus."[332] And, of course, new ads to sell the products.

Homeowners were assured that using the proper tools and chemicals would guarantee an attractive lawn and the leisure time to enjoy it. Whether the regimen of fertilizing, watering, aerating, mowing, and controlling weeds actually allowed more free time is questionable, but it did produce a beautiful yard.

In 1955 the Department of Horticulture at the University of Minnesota established a nursery of grasses commonly used in lawns at its Fruit Breeding Farm in Excelsior.[333] Several seed companies and national organizations like the Turf Research Foundation and the Better Lawn and Turf Institute contributed seeds. The reason for the new area of study, said R. J. Stadtherr of the university's horticulture department, was that "lawns . . . form an important part of the landscape setting for homes, apartments, factories, offices, churches and schools [and] involved many acres of land."[334] The economic factor was important as well. A 1953 California survey showed that over ninety million dollars was spent on lawn maintenance in California. "If one were to estimate the annual maintenance costs throughout the country," said Stadtherr, "one would reach astronomical figures."[335]

—•—

Anne and Ed Koempel's lovely perennial garden in Highland Park in St. Paul was a highlight of many area garden tours.

To homeowners, lawns were important not only for their beauty, but because they gave the family a place to set the lawn furniture and build a barbecue pit, a place to sunbathe and play catch. In the words of a 1956 Northrup King ad, "Yes, he wants grass . . . and in a hurry. What's more, he wants the kind of grass that can survive rough treatment . . . pounding feet, kids, dogs, more kids, wagons and trikes."[336] The outdoor living room of the thirties had become an open-air recreation area.

Outdoor relaxation was further enhanced by a new structure— the patio. Placed on ground level with the house so family members could come and go without climbing stairs, patios contributed to the feeling of ranch-house spaciousness. When well planned, said Hopkins nurseryman Russell H. Zakariasen, "they are the kind of practical and inviting places that the family really uses."[337]

The advent of patios meant a new kind of gardening because, said extension agent Hard, "plants are needed to make the patio homelike and colorful."[338] Articles in the *Minnesota Horticulturist* and local newspapers provided lists of suitable plants and growing instructions. Imaginative gardeners used containers of every description—redwood tubs, wooden rectangles on rollers, large clay pots, and glazed and decorated vases.

Inevitably, gardeners in older homes began to adopt aspects of the Minnesota/California style. Ponds were removed, patios installed. Rock gardens were replaced by picnic tables and pots of annuals. By 1965 it was difficult to find evidence of the arbors, water features, and rock gardens that had been so commonplace three decades earlier.

The vernacular landscape—broad lawn, pots of annuals around the patio—was characteristic of the era, but there were passionate gardeners as well. Especially noticeable for the first time were specialty gardeners—rose growers, dahlia experts, gladiola fanciers, African violet collectors. Everyone seemed to have an area of expertise. Articles in the *Minnesota Horticulturist*, a bellwether for gardening trends, discussed specific plants ("Iris Culture," "Roving with Roses," "Growing Gloxinias") more frequently than perennial borders or garden design. Membership in specialty organizations was at a new high; there were twenty-four Twin Cities chapters of the African Violet Society in 1953 and six hundred members of the Minnesota Rose Society in the late 1960s. Large regional and national shows spurred further interest. More than 83,000 people attended the gigantic National Rose Show at Dayton's in Minneapolis, October 27 and 28, 1952. Among the displays were a Christmas tree of two thousand red roses and a replica of Minnehaha Falls, rendered in roses with spiral eucalyptus simulating the water.[339]

Some gardeners accumulated impressive numbers of the plants in which they specialized. Amateur Dorothy Campbell fell in love with the Charlotte Armstrong rose in the fifties. Ultimately, her St. Louis Park garden would contain three hundred fifty roses. In addition, she wrote a column for *American Rose Magazine*, contributed to the *Minnesota Horticulturist*, and was frequently in demand as a speaker.[340]

Jerry Olson, a conductor for the Milwaukee Road, joined the Minnesota Rose Society in 1948 and won a second prize for his floribunda at the 1953 National Rose Show in Minneapolis. Eventually, he won so many awards that he gave up exhibiting, deciding it would be "more fun to teach others how they could win the ribbons too."[341] He came to know most of the nation's important rose breeders as well as being a highly touted judge and consulting rosarian himself. In 1994, in his seventies and still doing all his own gardening, Jerry had five hundred roses at his home in Bloomington. His credentials and awards may well make him the premier rose-gardener of the state.

Many men who had never grown flowers became enthusiastic specialists. Calvin Hopper near Mille Lacs "discovered" gladiola in 1951, when his wife sent in twenty-five cents and a coffee label for fifteen bulbs. Before this, said Hopper, "I didn't know one flower from another."[342] During the peak of his gardening days, Hopper and his wife planted some ten thousand bulbs. His hobby, he conceded, "had become quite consuming."[343]

The era had its share of versatile gardeners as well, people who seemed to grow many things well. Anne and Ed Koempel of St. Paul, created elaborate perennial borders based on English garden principles. Their Highland Park gardens in the 1960s included twenty-six varieties of peonies, single and double, and more than thirty varieties of iris, along with daylilies, roses, lupines, and chrysanthemums. Lilacs and azaleas added dazzling colors in spring.[344] For several decades the Koempel garden was a "must see" on area tours. The best thing about gardening, Anne once said, was the "peace and joy of the outdoors."[345]

Anne Koempel was as active in gardening organizations as she was in the garden; she found time to serve on many civic beautification committees, including the Clean Capital City Campaign and a committee to revitalize Kellogg Park. She was an enthusiastic mentor to new gardeners; many Twin Cities residents grew plants from her collection. The Koempels maintained their gardens until 1992 when advancing age forced them to move to a retirement home.

Bernard H. Ridder, publisher of the *St. Paul Pioneer Press* and *Dispatch*, with the help of a gardener, turned the grounds of his home on Lincoln Avenue in St. Paul into a spring and summer paradise. Every May fifteen thousand tulips, great beds in every color and shape, bloomed against a backdrop of flowering apple trees and purple lilacs.[346] Hundreds of roses followed; Peace, Charlotte Armstrong, Sister Therese, and Crimson Glory were among the favorites. Lilies, peonies, iris, gladiolus, chrysanthemums, and a "Saucer" magnolia were just some of the plants that filled in the remainder of the season.

In an unusual gesture, the Ridders made their grounds more than a private haven, opening them to the public throughout the fifties and sixties. One Sunday in 1952, at the peak of tulip-watching, twenty-five-thousand visitors came through the gates.[347] Other days, school children were bussed in, garden clubs toured, or individual guests strolled through.

The Ridders used their garden to test new varieties and growing techniques, then reported their findings in the *St. Paul Sunday Pioneer Press*. For years Joe Steigauf, the Ridders' gardener, wrote a weekly column, "In Our Garden—What we are doing now and how we do it." Ridder himself took over the column in 1957. When readers questioned the publisher's ability to write on flowers and gardens, Ridder assured them that he was "only an amateur expressing opinions."[348] He relied on others for technical information, especially local rose expert Richard Wilcox and University horticulturist Dr. Robert Phillips, both of whom wrote gardening advice for the paper. Besides, Ridder added, "while there is much that a publisher does not understand, there is nothing which he cannot explain."[349] Ridder lived into his eighties and even in his last years was eager to guide visitors through his gardens.

Many gardeners began to rely on the services of landscape designers. The staffs of companies like Bachman's in Minneapolis and Kelley and Kelley Nursery in Long Lake were ready to help customers. Independent landscape architects found a growing clientele. Over the fifty-year period in which he practiced, Edmund J. Phelps of Orono was one of the most significant talents in the state. His clients included many prominent families in the Twin Cities, among them the Cargills, Pillsburys, Daytons, Hamms, and Pipers in Minneapolis and the Ordways and Weyerhaeusers in St. Paul. He also did work for the Congdons in Duluth and customers in Rochester and Winona.[350]

Extensive as his business was, Phelps's entrance into the field was almost accidental. Born into a wealthy family in 1890, "Eddie" grew up in Ferndale on Lake Minnetonka. Each year he spent a month with his parents in Europe. His connection with the continent remained intense; he was fluent in French at age ten and later developed a lifelong devotion to France. Shortly after Phelps graduated from Yale, World War I broke out, and he headed to Europe to help his adopted country. He was a volunteer ambulance driver in France and later a lieutenant in the French Foreign Legion.[351] Even in the midst of war, he was a

Smithsonian Institution, Archives of American Gardens, Garden Club of America

keen observer of the beauty around him, noting in his diary, "The wild-flowers are brilliant and luxuriant everywhere."[352] For his heroic service, France awarded Phelps its highest military honor, the *Croix de Guerre*.

As a young man, Phelps went into the family insurance business briefly until illness intervened, and a family friend suggested landscape architecture at Harvard. Moving his wife Katherine and their child to Massachusetts, he spent three years studying his craft, arriving back in Minneapolis in 1927, just before the Depression. Though his family subsequently lost much of its fortune, Eddie managed to ply his trade even in the worst years. He hired Louise P. Mealey as assistant and a crew of workmen to execute his designs, which reflected the styles of earlier estate gardens.

According to Peter Olin, director of the Minnesota Landscape Arboretum, Phelps was "a master at handling proportion, scale, form and relationships between elements in the landscape; he created gardens of beauty and visual balance."[353] He had a preference for

formal landscapes and he had his favorite plants—delphiniums, roses, peonies, and lilacs, but he also used wildflowers in several landscapes.

By the late 1930s Phelps was handling a significant portion of the estate work in Minnesota. Some of his more notable projects included Southways, the John S. Pillsbury estate on Lake Minnetonka; Stillpond, the large French chateau of Rufus Rand, now the world headquarters of Cargill, Inc.; Old Orchard, the Leonard Carpenter property on Lake Minnetonka; and Green Trees, the George Halpin estate in Orono.[354]

The Halpin commission, begun in 1951, gave Phelps the opportunity to work the way he preferred—in concert with the architect from planning to completion. People often think the contractor arranges the grading, said Phelps, "and all I do is plant a few pansies, but grading is fundamental. Everything depends on it."[355]

Louise Mealey designed the clover-shaped English garden on the Halpin property. Phelps landscaped the rest, beginning with an informal entrance of fieldstone pillars, followed by a circular drive, statuary and formal plantings for the main entrance. Tucked in a corner by the house was a secluded garden, where two hundred roses were bordered by dwarf Japanese yew and backed by a dramatic stand of arborvitae. The terraced front garden with fountains and statues provided a view of Smith Bay in Lake Minnetonka.[356]

After her husband's death, Margaret Halpin willed the estate to the Minneapolis Society of Fine Arts. In 1979, one year after she died, a series of fund-raising events involved the house and gardens, then the property was sold to a developer. The extensive grounds were divided into lots for several home sites.

Edmund Phelps was ninety years old when he died in 1980; that he had attained a great age, he implied, had something to do with his occupation. In memory of his accomplishments, a number of his friends, including Mrs. John S. (Eleanor) Pillsbury, Mrs. Folwell (Olivia) Coan, and Mrs. Carl (Helen) Jones, created the Edmund J. Phelps Memorial Fund to provide scholarships for students in the School of Architecture and Landscape Architecture at the University of Minnesota.[357]

Mrs. John S. Pillsbury's garden on Lake Minnetonka was designed by Edmund Phelps.

PUBLIC SPACES

The establishment of a landscape arboretum will increase the interest in horticulture,
add to the beauty of the state, and enrich the lives of its citizens.

Mrs. Edmund Phelps, 1956.[358]

Public spaces in the post-war decades were an interesting mix of the traditional and innovative. New public gardens, like the Veterans Memorial Rose Garden at the State Capitol, were most often patterned after historic models. Corporate and institutional landscapes, however, included the work of nationally-known modernists like Daniel Kiley, Hideo Sasaki, and Lawrence Halprin. Their projects included Sasaki's garden for Lutheran Brotherhood in downtown Minneapolis, Kiley's master plans for Carleton College and Blake School, and Halprin's design for Nicollet Mall.

Modernism as expressed in the landscape suggested a visual language that was clean, honest, and unadorned. Gardens were simple in line and relied heavily on low-maintenance plants. Landscape designs did not set out to decorate the site, but simply to reveal its hidden essence.

Designers like Dan Kiley found Minnesota receptive to their work. Since the mid-1950s the Boston-born, Harvard rebel has planned about fifty projects in the state. His style, according *Landscape Architecture*, is typified by "a clear, clean geometric order and continuous flow of space."[359] Explaining his philosophy, Kiley said in a 1985 interview: "Man has always made more or less straight lines. Take the Vermont farm, Africa, everywhere it's the same. Whenever you look from the air, everything is geometric.

The Knot Garden at the Minnesota Landscape Arboretum has been an inspiration for home gardeners since 1980.

Hideo Sasaki's garden, designed for Lutheran Brotherhood in Minneapolis, provides a tranquil respite from city life.

Lynn Steiner

Chris Faust

I have always thought it was some kind of superficial, sentimental, romantic corruption of man's culture on the land when he gets cute and throws trees around in a disorganized way."[360]

Kiley's local work has included the highly visible—the archbishop's residence in St. Paul, the urban design for much of the University of Minnesota's West Bank expansion in the 1960s—in addition to the relatively private, such as an entrance for the George Pillsbury home on Ferndale Road. Kiley also served on the Capitol Area Planning Board.

Born in California, Sasaki attended universities there before transferring to the University of Illinois, where he graduated with highest honors in 1946. He earned his master's degree in landscape architecture from Harvard University in 1948 and returned there in 1953 as chair of the Landscape Architecture Department. At Harvard his exceptional talents for organization and communication began to blossom. Sasaki started a landscaping design firm which eventually employed three hundred people, forcing him to leave Harvard and concentrate on private projects.[361]

Sasaki has worked on small and large-scale renovations, urban design developments, and open civic space. Important national commissions include the John Deere headquarters in Moline, Illinois, and Boston's Copley Square. His designs are recognized by their strong geometric forms and rich plant textures.[362]

In Minnesota, Sasaki's gem of a garden for Lutheran Brotherhood at 201 South 7th Street in Minneapolis, remains an elegant reminder of the best modernism has to offer. Fluid geometry, deep greens, broadly curved plantings, and a sense of enclosure create a wonderful tranquility, the ideal foil for a busy downtown. Within this peaceful uniformity, Sasaki has placed small visual delights: a textured stone bollard, ivy tendrils on a step. The spot, since 1981 the headquarters of Minnegasco, wears well; its smooth hedges and strong lines make it as compelling in the 1990s as it was thirty years ago when it was created.

It's curious," said garden writer Candace Wheeler, "how large a space the rose idea occupies in the world."[363] She could well have been talking about post-war Minnesota, where roses were the focus of public and private gardens.

Roses require special coddling even in moderate climates. To look their best, they need consistent water, extra fertilizer,

treatment for diseases, and deadheading. In Minnesota, they must have special care to make it safely through the winter. To place roses in a public setting takes a real commitment, because of all flowers, they may be the most labor-intensive.

Roses, however, have a history. No other flower has loomed so large in human affections. They grew in ancient Egypt; they were cultivated in Plato's Greece. Christians found symbolic links between the rose and the Virgin.[364] Poets and artists have found them irresistible. Daisies may be delightful, violets charming, but when we speak of love, when we pay tribute, we give the rose.

So it is not surprising that several public rose gardens opened in Minnesota between 1955 and 1970, all initiated by private citizens and often tended by volunteers—labors of love and gifts to the community.

The earliest, the Veterans Memorial Rose Garden was begun by Thomas W. Walsh of St. Paul, a veteran of World Wars I and II and a member of both the American and Minnesota Rose societies. The garden on the Capitol grounds was planned as a living memorial to Minnesota veterans, the first of its kind "in all the 48 states,"[365] according to a newspaper article at the time.

D.R. Martin

The Duluth Rose Garden in 1994.

Walsh headed a committee that included other rose fanciers, such as Bernard H. Ridder, publisher of the *Pioneer Press;* George Luxton, a writer for the *Minneapolis Tribune;* and Professor Robert Phillips of the University of Minnesota Department of Horticulture. Thousands of dollars in contributions came from veterans' groups, rose societies, garden clubs, and interested individuals.

Construction of the large garden on the Capitol Approach area began in October 1955, with Governor Orville Freeman turning the first shovelful of earth. The garden, he said, was a "memorial to veterans from this state and from all states who gave their lives so that freedom [could] continue on the face of the earth."[366] The following summer, two thousand roses, grouped by color and type, were planted, and the garden was opened to the public. Though on state property, costs and upkeep were to come from private sources.

The committee realized that a dedicated rosarian was needed to keep the flowers in excellent shape. In Albert I. Nelson of south Minneapolis they found the ideal person. "He was a real rose man," said Hazel Sweeney of Minneapolis, past editor of the Rose Society bulletin. "Not only did he have a large rose garden himself, with lots of unusual roses, but he had the commitment and knowledge to keep the grounds in wonderful condition."[367]

Nelson gave devoted service through the mid-1960s and kept the gardens in peak condition. By 1969 private funds were exhausted and the garden was turned over to the state.

"At times, there is not enough staff to give the roses the attention they deserve," said attendant Sheila Ubell. "The garden is a great place to work. So many people come by and tell me how wonderful it is to have roses on the Capitol grounds."[368]

Winona had its rose enthusiasts as well. Local dentist Dr. Clay Rohrer helped organize the Winona Rose Society and persuaded the city to develop a rose garden in Lake Park, with Sugar Loaf Mountain and Lake Winona as background.

The first year (1957), the Park Department bought fifty bushes, but Rohrer built on that number steadily.[369] He convinced nurseries, such as the national suppliers Jackson and Perkins, to donate roses and encouraged local people to present bushes as memorials.

By 1971 the garden included over one thousand rose bushes and was viewed by nearly twenty thousand tourists a year. In 1975 Dr. Rohrer gave the city $2,000, which was to be invested, and the income "used for the betterment of the garden and park at Lake Winona."[370] That summer the garden was dedicated and named in Dr. Rohrer's honor. Today, it continues to attract locals and visitors.

In Duluth, Mrs. John Klints, a native of Latvia, longed for a chance to show her appreciation to her adopted country. No better way, she decided, than to build an elegant rose garden, laid out like those she'd known in Europe. She chose a spot in Leif Erickson Park overlooking the magnificent blue waters of Lake Superior, and enlisted the aid of fellow rose lovers.[371]

The finished garden, opened for visitors in 1965, contained over two thousand roses planted in gentle curves. Hybrid teas, grandifloras, floribundas, climbers, and old-fashioned varieties were clustered by hue around an antique horse fountain. Volunteers from the Duluth Rose Society tended the roses for over twenty-five years, helping to earn the prestigious "Public Show Garden of America" award.[372]

In 1990 freeway construction displaced the flowers, but Duluthians received a new site, even more stunning than the original. The summer of 1994 the Minnesota Department of Transportation, the city of Duluth, and the Parks Department completed the six-acre garden, which features two thousand roses arranged in four circles and two long beds. Once again, the flowers, the setting, and the garden design have made the rose garden a premier attraction.

Gardens in every corner of the state are important, beloved parts of their communities, that give Minnesotans a chance to observe cultivated beauty up close. But the Minnesota Landscape Arboretum in Chanhassen provides the opportunity to garden on a grand scale. There, horticulturists can try plants of borderline hardiness and test varieties for beauty and disease-resistance. Visitors can experience crabapple blossoms in May, perennial flowers all summer, the blaze of maples each fall, and snow-covered firs and pines in winter. The number of species and cultivars is estimated to be over four thousand.

In one morning, visitors can view a bog, pond, prairie, and northern woodlands, in addition to research collections and landscaped areas. Cultivated landscapes, such as the medieval knot garden, the cool fern walk, the elegant rose garden, and *Seisui-Tei* (the Japanese garden of Pure Water) cross centuries and countries. The DeVos Home Demonstration Gardens display scaled-down spaces comparable to most homeowners' yards.

The idea for the arboretum was a bold one, requiring prodigious effort to bring it about. The first documented request for a state-financed arboretum dates to 1875. Writing in the *St. Paul Daily Press,* Lyman Ford called for the university to develop an arboretum or botanical garden.[374]

Not until September 6, 1958, however, did the arboretum become a reality. Initial steps for the center were made by a group within the Men's Garden Club of Minneapolis.[375] The men

approached the Minnesota State Horticultural Society and requested that a planning committee be appointed. Eight people met in January 1955. The group included professional horticulturist Dr. Leon Snyder, head of the University of Minnesota's Horticultural Science Department; nurseryman Vincent K. Bailey of Bailey Nurseries; and passionate gardeners Archie Flack of the Men's Garden Club of Minneapolis and Anne Koempel of the Garden Club of Ramsey County and the Minnesota Garden and Flower Society.

By March the quest for an arboretum was official and the newly appointed committee began searching for a site and collecting funds. In June 1956, with money provided by Mrs. Grace B. Dayton, an option was taken on one hundred sixty acres across from the

New spring growth frames the Snyder Education and Research Building at the Minnesota Landscape Arboretum—Minnesota's premier garden.

university's Fruit Breeding Farm in Chanhassen. By the fall of 1957 the Lake Minnetonka Garden Club had raised the $35,000 necessary to purchase the land, and the Hill Family Foundation had provided a research grant of $60,000. The following year the horticultural society transferred the arboretum land and funds to the University of Minnesota, after being assured by the board of regents that the arboretum would be a continuing part of its mission.

Dr. Snyder, center, was named director in 1958. Even though he continued as chair of the Horticultural Science Department and superintendent of the Fruit Breeding Farm during the first ten years, Dr. Snyder placed great emphasis on the arboretum's growth. That he managed each post so well is a testament to his vision and dedication. Mervin Eisel, one of his former students, explained: "He worked about a triple shift. He spent his weekends at the arboretum. We had a weekend crew, of which Dr. Snyder was a working member. Except when the Gophers had a home game, he recognized no holiday or hours."[376] His wife Vera said it simply: "Leon lived his horticulture."[377]

Minnesotans are the beneficiaries of his devotion. During his tenure, the arboretum evolved from a bit of rolling countryside to an impressive 576-acre landscape laboratory with a wonderful network of roads and paths, while retaining existing wet-lands, woods, and prairie."[378]

Using designs of landscape architects Hare and Hare of Kansas City, Dr. Snyder placed new trees and shrubs around the native plantings. He also created a prairie with help from the Russell Bennetts of Wayzata, and added a woodland wildflower garden with funds from the Dayton family to honor their mother, Grace B. Dayton.

"Leon had the idea that all the arboretum was a garden, both what was created and what existed," explained arboretum director Peter Olin in 1994. "This was really a contrast to the man-dominated landscapes created by Kiley, Sasaki, and Halprin."[379]

Added under his guidance were the handsome Snyder Education and Research Building, the excellent Andersen Horticultural Library

Minnesota Landscape Arboretum

(sponsored by former governor Elmer Andersen), the azalea hybridization program, and a number of special gardens and habitats. "It was Leon Snyder's vision that the people of Minnesota have a place to view hardy trees, shrubs, and perennials in a landscape setting," said Olin. "In such a display, people could relate a particular plant to their own home settings."[380]

In his quest for an exemplary facility, Dr. Snyder had the help of many Minnesotans. Individuals and garden clubs worked long hours and gave generously so the building and programs might be developed. In 1962, when it became apparent that more land was needed, the St. Paul Garden Club speedily raised $45,000. Later, other benefactors contributed at different times to expand the original parcel. Inspired fund-raising spearheaded by John Morgan of Gem Lake helped make the Snyder Education and Research Building possible. "The arboretum is really Minnesota's garden," said Olin, "built with private resources rather than government grants."[381]

In 1976 Dr. Snyder retired as arboretum director, but remained an active member of the horticultural community. He continued his weekly newspaper column for the *Minneapolis Tribune* and his appearances on WCCO radio. Mervin Eisel, who was in charge of arboretum classes, said later that Dr. Snyder never refused a request to teach a session.[382]

Books about Minnesota gardening have been relatively few, but during his retirement Dr. Snyder wrote six which have been singularly helpful: *Gardening in the Upper Midwest, Trees and Shrubs for Northern Gardens, How Does Your Garden Grow?, Flowers for Northern Gardens, A Minnesota Gardener's Companion* (as co-author), and *Native Plants for Northern Gardens.*

Snyder was honored time and again for his accomplishments. The Men's Garden Club of America gave him its gold medal; the National Council of State Garden Clubs, a silver. Both the American Association of Nurserymen and the American Horticultural Society awarded him their highest honors. In 1975 he won the American Association of Botanic Gardens and Arboreta Award for outstanding arboretum development.

He took a private dream, said long-time friend and pupil Jane McKinnon, one "many thought impossible [and] enlarged Minnesota's vision enough to inspire hundreds of people to share generously their time and resources."[383]

D.R. Martin

THE TRADE

A FOOTNOTE TO HISTORY

1850 - 1990

—◆—

Apple blossom time in the Pepin Heights Orchard in Lake City, Minnesota. Pepin Heights is one of many commercial apple growers in southeastern Minnesota.

H O W   C O L D   I S   I T ?

It is quite surprising to mark the mistaken opinions prevalent about us at the East. We have sometimes been referred to as if our climate was as cold as Greenland, and only adapted to polar bears and ice-palaces.

American Association of Nurserymen, 1891.[384]

Up to now, Minnesota's garden story has been concerned almost entirely with the amateur side of gardening. It would be incomplete without reference to the booming flower trade and tireless breeders who brought the state prominence in difficult circumstances.

Minnesota winters are notoriously bitter; the growing season is short and rainfall variable. This information is obvious, but in any discussion of horticulture it bears repeating. Given such difficult weather, the state's record in producing a great wealth of horticultural resources in a little over a century has few parallels in history.

Various institutions and individuals distinguished themselves internationally by the mid-twentieth century. Among them was Carl Fischer of St. Charles, the world's leading hybridizer of gladiola. His most famous introduction is Friendship, of which millions of bulbs have been sold worldwide, more than any other gladiolus.[385] Northrup King Seed Company had become the dominant supplier of seed packets in stores and the largest

general seed house in the world. By the late 1940s Wedge Nursery in Albert Lea was the world's major grower of French hybrid lilacs. Between 1919 and 1953 the University of Minnesota's Horticulture Department developed 124 new varieties of fruits, vegetables, and flowers, including Haralson and Beacon apples, the Latham raspberry, Red Lake currant, and many garden chrysanthemums.[386] By 1970 Bailey Nurseries in Newport was one of the largest growers and wholesale suppliers of nursery stock for the northern tier of states. Clearly, Minnesota's horticulture trade had achieved national status.

The situation a century earlier gave no hint of the success that was to follow. Indeed, early Minnesotans were frequently taunted about growing conditions in the state.

The Growers Association of St. Paul had a yearly display at the state fair. Lavish exhibits like this one in 1905 helped build confidence in Minnesota's food production capabilities.

"What can be raised away up there in Siberia?" their East Coast friends asked. In rejoinder, the *Minnesota Republican* in 1855 ran a series of articles describing fine corn, good soil, large turnips: "If you're in doubt, come and see for yourself. Minnesota challenges the world to raise vegetables of equal size and flavor."[387]

Civic leaders understood that successful horticulture was essential to a prosperous state. But growing vegetables was one matter; raising fruit and delicate ornamentals was quite another. Abundant wild fruit and flowers could only go so far in filling the need.

"The king of fruit," the apple, was what the settlers wanted first. Early diaries and newspaper stories record their attempts to grow apples from back East. Their efforts were rarely successful. This account in *The History of Freeborn County* is typical:

The honor of establishing the first good-sized orchard in the county belongs to the Rev. Isaac W. McReynolds . . . who planted apple seed in 1858. These trees in due time came on and bore considerable fruit, so that by the year 1870 he was harvesting crops of fifty to seventy-five bushels. . . . However, like most of the early seedling orchards that were grown from promiscuous seed gathered from eastern orchards, they carried with them in their ancestry no special adaptation to the climate of the West, and one by one they succumbed to severe winters and drouthy summers, till at the end of twenty years very little was left to show for the effort that had been put forth.[388]

The two men most responsible for Minnesota's successful apple crops were John Harris and Peter M. Gideon, a settler on Lake Minnetonka.

For a time, the problems seemed insurmountable. Horace Greeley's was not the only voice to declare that "you can't raise apples in Minnesota." Harris, who has been called "the father of orchards in Minnesota," reported the reaction of other farmers at the 1866 state fair when he and Colonel D. A. Roberts of St. Paul proposed a fruit growers' society. "We were looked upon by many," said Harris, "with serious suspicions of our sanity, but our hope and enthusiasm became contagious and has extended to every part of the state."[389]

Peter Gideon, like Harris, had a determined spirit. In 1853, shortly after arriving from Ohio with his wife Wealth and their children, Gideon began experimental plantings of numerous varieties of apple, peach, and cherry trees, plus apple and pear seeds.[390] For nine years he added to his collection, only to discover at the end of the tenth year that Minnesota winters had killed all but the seedlings of Siberian crabs.

Impoverished and discouraged, with a large family to support, Gideon continued to display the "hope and enthusiasm" to which Harris referred. Taking his last eight dollars, Gideon wrote to Maine for apple seeds and scion wood (grafting material). In need of clothing, he sewed together two old vests and succeeded in making himself a winter suit, "more odd than ornamental,"[391] by his own account.

Gideon's persistence was rewarded. From his Siberian crab and crosses, in 1868 he developed the Wealthy apple. Gideon's apple trees survived the bitter winter in 1872-73, proving that the variety could successfully be grown throughout the northern United States and Canada.[392] His experience was also valuable in showing that most eastern and southern trees were not hardy here and, more importantly, that by growing and testing seedlings, new varieties could be established.

Gideon's experimental efforts were not unique. Hundreds of other men spent the pioneer era working in relative isolation to find hardy varieties. Swedish immigrant Andrew Peterson, whose forty-year diary served as a source of information for Vilhelm Moberg's novels—*The Emigrants, Unto a Good Land,* and *The Last Letter Home*—describes the long years of work and bouts with the weather in his daily records, which began in 1855.[393]

Peterson's life was a Minnesota rags-to-riches story. His success was apparent by March 1873, when he wrote: "This winter I have grafted 404 apple trees, 13 pear trees, 30 plum trees, and 12 cherry trees."[394] Increasingly, people came to buy his plants.

Certainly, there were setbacks. On July 30, 1878, he wrote:

. . . it started to rain, and then it hailed. I have never seen anything like it . . . but the worst of all was that the bark was scaled off the apple trees. In other words, everything in the path of the storm was destroyed.[395]

But Peterson persevered and began describing his experiments for the *Minnesota Horticulturist*. He was especially happy with his Russian apples. In his last published essay, dated 1893, Peterson stated that he had planted over one hundred apple trees from Russia and been successful with a handful.[396]

St. John's Abbey Archives

***Father John Katzner at St. John's in Collegeville
turned his hand to hybridizing fruit.***

After Peterson died in 1898, Professor Samuel Green from the University of Minnesota commented on the importance of Peterson's experiments. "His work, in fact, amounted to his carrying on at his own expense and in a most careful way for more than a quarter of a century what amounted to a private experiment station."[397]

Individual efforts were important as fruit-growing began, but to make great strides, a coordinated system was needed. To that end, the Minnesota Horticultural Society in 1878 secured passage of an act establishing the Minnesota Fruit Farm, an experiment station in Hennepin County. Peter Gideon was superintendent until 1889, when personality clashes between Gideon and university administrators led to its closing.[398] Though short-lived, the venture was significant because it was the first tax-supported fruit-breeding station in the country.

In 1883 the state horticultural society itself established a series of experiment stations for testing ornamentals and vegetables as well as fruit. Results of their experiments were published twice a year in the *Minnesota Horticulturist*.

The devotion of Father John Katzner, superintendent of the Collegeville station at St. John's University from 1908 to 1924, was typical among researchers at these stations. After poor health forced him to retire from a forty-year career teaching music at the college, Katzner turned to horticulture. His work in beautifying the campus and breeding hardy plants brought attention and fame to St. John's and to Katzner. Father John experimented with more than two hundred varieties of apples, sixty plums, thirty-five grapes (the Alpha grape brought him regional prominence), and ten cherries, and wrote up meticulous reports for the *Minnesota Horticulturist*.[399]

Time and again, Father John's reports turned on the weather. In 1907 he commented: "Last winter was rather a severe one. . . . The weather was so unfavorable that the vegetation was about four weeks behind time."[400] Two years later he reported: "This spring . . . we had many cold rains. . . . Then came the severe, protracted drought."[401] Despite setbacks, Father Katzner continued to cross varieties and keep records of his findings. His work took time, he said, and so "a farmer could not do this," but his intention was "to work for the future for our locality, without despising the present returns on the orchard."[402]

Members of the horticultural society recognized the value of having the University of Minnesota take responsibility for plant breeding, and persuaded the legislature to appropriate funds for a new tax-supported facility. In 1908 land was purchased for the university's Fruit Breeding Farm, which years later became the Horticultural Research Center.[403] Most of the research was aimed at breeding fruits, though the farm also developed ornamentals for the home garden, flowering crabs, dogwoods, and azaleas.[404]

Minnesota's climate has continued to be the driving force behind many university introductions. Before 1941, for example, there were few chrysanthemums that could be grown in northern gardens. Autumn frosts, which come early in Minnesota, usually killed the buds or flowers before they could be enjoyed. Dr. L. E. Longley of the university's horticulture department developed a breeding program to remedy that, using the earliest-flowering varieties from other parts of the country. In his years at the university (1936-1949), Dr. Longley introduced more than thirty varieties, including Minnpink and Autumn Beauty.[405] After Longley's retirement, Dr. Richard Widmer continued the work. Their efforts have made the chrysanthemum a reliable favorite in Minnesota gardens.

Azaleas presented a special challenge to Minnesota horticulturists. None grow wild here; they've never adapted to the state's climate. Still, their exotic beauty has induced gardeners and nurserymen to put various strains on trial, and after mild winters, some bloomed well. But following a hard winter, imported azaleas died or failed to blossom. So, when horticulturists hybridized azaleas that could grow in Minnesota gardens, there was cause for celebration.

In 1957 Al Johnson of the Horticultural Research Center made a successful cross. Having worked at the Arnold Arboretum at Harvard, Johnson was familiar with the rose-shell azalea (*Rhododendron primophyllum*) that grows in the Appalachian mountains. Though a small plant with small flowers, it blooms consistently after low temperatures and has a fine fragrance. This he crossed with the large-flowered *Azalea mollis*. The resulting hybrid (Northern Lights) carried the best of both parents—large, fragrant blossoms and true bud hardiness.[406] Since Johnson's initial introduction, Dr. Harold Pellett has worked with the strain, adding the wide range of colors now available commercially.

Many new plants are in store for Minnesota if Dr. Pellett has his way. As director of the Center for the Development of Hardy Landscape Plants at the Minnesota Landscape Arboretum, Pellett is developing superior plants that will stand tough winters, droughty summers. His innovative program coordinates the research activities of institutions around the globe. "He is in the forefront of plant breeders," explained Peter Olin, director of the Minnesota Landscape Arboretum. "Most plant breeding involves crops, such as corn, that

reproduce quickly. To see the results of work such as Pellett is doing takes fifteen to twenty years."[407] Dr. Pellett has already developed a wide range of colors in azaleas (pink, orchid, apricot, and white), in addition to a number of new plant varieties such as Northern Sun Forsythia, Cardinal Dogwood, Freedom Honeysuckle, two red maples, and several other ornamentals.

The future has "unlimited possibilities," Dr. Pellett predicts. "How fast we can improve landscape plants depends on our resources and, of course, time." Some plants to look for are better small ornamental trees with good fall color; hardier, disease-resistant roses; and more shapely azaleas in the complete color range. "In general, we can develop plants that are better adapted to a wide range of conditions."[408]

Without a thriving nursery business to market their introductions, Minnesota hybrids might have languished. But from its earliest days, the state has had its share of dedicated commercial growers.

Because new towns needed horticultural resources, nurseries often opened soon after the town was platted. Faribault Nursery advertised itself as "Minnesota's oldest and best," listing its start-up date as 1856. Fairbault was recognized as a township in the same year. In 1854, just three years after Lyman Ford opened his nursery, Wyman Elliott moved to Minneapolis from Maine and became the city's first market gardener.[409] His operation, near the present intersection of Franklin and Chicago Avenues, grew rapidly. By 1866 Elliott had a greenhouse, in addition to a nursery and seed business.

In 1874 the state horticultural society's annual report listed thirty-seven florists and nurserymen. No doubt, there were others not affiliated with the society. According to the report, Minneapolis had four nurseries; Faribault and Litchfield each had three. Both Mankato and Blue Earth had their own nurseries, as did Money Creek (population 609) and Brownsville (1,589).[410]

Nurseries and seed companies knew they were in a tough business. Most emphasized their familiarity with Minnesota's climate and how they triumphed over it. Typical was the statement by O. J. Brand, proprietor in Faribault, who announced on the cover of his 1895 catalogue, "Tried by 28 Years of Minnesota Climate." Inside, he added to his credentials:

Born on the Snowy Hills of Lewis County, northern New York,

where six feet of snow on a level was the usual winter covering,

I learned . . . to combat with climatic conditions.[411]

FIRST PRIZE ASTERS, MINNESOTA STATE FAIR.

SEE PAGE 5.

1904 FLOWER SEEDS.

JESSIE R. PRIOR. SEEDSWOMAN.

LIPPINCOTT FLOWER SEEDS

MISS C.H. LIPPINCOTT. MINNEAPOLIS.MINN.

CHOICE FLOWER SEEDS

CALIFORNIA GIANT COSMOS, MIXED

PKT. 75 SEEDS 5¢

DOROTHY

1903 MISS EMMA V. WHITE, 818 NICOLLET AVE. MINNEAPOLIS, MINN.

Andersen Horticultural Library, William Seaman

**The three seedswomen of Minneapolis pioneered
in selling flower seeds through the mail.**

Nurseries experimented often to develop a wider range of plants for their customers. Jewell Nursery in Lake City, one of the region's largest, devoted hundreds of acres to growing "new and untried sorts." Those that were "found too tender for this climate or lacking in quality [were] consigned to the brush heap."[412] Jewell, led by president J. B. Underwood, grew millions of seedlings for timber claims and windbreaks, fields of roses, a large variety of ornamental and fruiting plants, and a vineyard containing three thousand plants.

Nurseries have continued to develop sturdier, more beautiful varieties. In the 1990s Julius Wadekamp of Elk River hybridizes lilies, including ones chosen by Princess Diana and Prince Charles for their wedding.[413] Breeders at Bailey Nurseries in Newport have been working to upgrade shrub roses. Using several hardy strains, they are breeding to improve flower quality, disease resistance, and hardiness.

Early firms specialized in fruits, with ornamentals making up a smaller portion of the business. One exception was Wedge Nursery, probably Minnesota's oldest family-run nursery. Named Echo Farm Nursery in 1878 by founder Clarence Wedge, the firm sold fruit trees and other plants.[414] After Wedge's son Robert joined in 1906, they shifted to eighty percent ornamentals and the remainder in windbreaks and fruit trees. In 1933, when Robert's son Don went to work at the company, the Wedges added landscaping to their list of specialties. By the 1960s, with third- and fourth-generation Wedges in charge, the firm had gained an international reputation for the propagation and production of over two hundred varieties of lilacs. In the late twentieth century, there were still Wedges at the helm.

At the turn of the century, mail-order business witnessed spectacular growth due to the development of the U.S. Postal Service and the railroads. Nurseries and seed companies found the mail a great boon. A 1906 *Minneapolis Journal* story, "Mails are crowded with Flowers", claimed that

hardy northern seeds are in great demand and Minneapolis is the

center from which they are distributed. Seed packets are a heavy item

in the outgoing mail at the post office. . . . Foreman John Meyer of

the mailing room says that over a thousand seed packages pass

through his department every day.[415]

Three Minneapolis women—Carrie Lippincott, Jessie Prior, and Emma White—began issuing seed catalogues. Lippincott was the first, sending out her initial offering in 1891 and proclaiming herself "Pioneer Seedswoman of America." Her 1895 catalogue included a quote from the *Minneapolis Tribune*: "Miss C. H. Lippincott came to Minneapolis eight years ago from Philadelphia where she had grown up among flowers and plants, with relatives actively engaged in floriculture."[416] Belying the current notion of the passive Victorian female, the quote continued:

The fact that a woman has grown up so successful in a short time and in the Northwest, speaks another word for the energetic end-of-the-century feminine, who is ill-content to fold her hands and let others feed and clothe her, or, having a living to make does not hesitate to go about it.[417]

Business boomed. In 1891 Lippincott filled six thousand orders; by 1896 the number was one hundred fifty thousand. As the first woman in the flower seed industry, Lippincott made the most of her gender, aiming her dainty lithographed catalogues at female readers. "My friends have urged me to print my latest picture because a number of seedsmen (shall I call them men?) have assumed women's names in order to sell seeds,"[418] stated her 1899 offering.

The imposters to which she refers could not have included Emma W. White, who in addition to running a seed business was president of the Women's Auxiliary of the Minnesota State Horticultural Society. Perhaps the culprit was Jessie R. Prior, whose flower business had the same address as her husband's law firm, and in fact, was in Joseph Prior's name until 1901.[419]

For whatever reason, Prior's business folded first, in 1907. White continued until 1919 when she sold the company to W. H. Bofferding. Lippincott enjoyed the longest run, finally going out of business as a florist in 1934.

Gender, not weather, was the seedswomens' stock-in-trade. But rival seedsmen Northrup, Braslan & Company (later Northrup King) made the most of their North Country connections, naming their seeds "Polar Brand." "Northern grown seeds," said their ads, "are early, more hardy and more productive than any other."

Jesse Northrup and Charles P. Braslan came to Minneapolis from the East in 1884, convinced that northern seed was superior and, moreover, that Minneapolis was *the* natural distribution point in an agricultural region with great promise. Their small firm opened its doors at 22 Hennepin Avenue on Bridge Square.[420] By 1917 the hugely successful company built an enormous headquarters and warehouse, with ten acres of floor space, at 1500 Jackson N. E. The main plant could accommodate fifty-three rail cars and was shipping seeds to retailers across the country.

For much of the first half of the twentieth century, Northrup King's large sales force personally visited every retailer. Each summer a crew made up primarily of college students took to the roads to check on seed displays, collect money, and ship back displays and unused seed.[421]

On their own and in the far reaches of the country, these young men had to cope with overheated engines, full boarding houses, and difficult retailers. Perhaps it was the chance of operating a car all summer or the opportunity to travel, but many were hooked on the experience and signed on for repeat seasons. One of these young men was Cedric Adams, the nationally-known columnist and radio comentator; another became mayor of Minneapolis. And they also numbered among their ranks future preachers, doctors, lawyers, and dentists.

"Those were glorious days," Adams recalled. "Up to that time, I had never been west of Willmar, so . . . four summers of paid sightseeing among the rocks and rills of our Wonderful West was wonderful stuff."[422]

His summers on the road between 1922 and 1926 sealed Adams's fate as a writer, for "when the rest of the salesmen were going to the movies or dating the waitress,"[423] he went up to his room and typed. Most of his writing was correspondence to Mox Lindquist, editor of Northrup King's newsletter, *Seed Bag*. When up against a deadline, Lindquist would include one of Cedric's letters and give him a byline. "There was something very exciting about seeing your name in print," Adams said, "so I became a writer."[424]

Climate has had a dual role in Minnesota's horticultural history. Harsh conditions have certainly limited what could be grown here. Still, the very severity of the climate has steeled horticulturists and gardeners in their determination to succeed.

Northrup, Braslan, Goodwin and Co., now
Northrup King and Company, originated in Minneapolis.
Jesse Northrup stands second from left with employees in front
of the retail store at 10-12 Hennepin Avenue.

Emphasizing their northern connections,
Northrup, Braslan & Co. advertised "Polar Brand Seeds"
in one of the first color posters. The building in the
background is the company's second headquarters at
Bridge Square on Hennepin Avenue in Minneapolis.

D.R. Martin

In 1921 Judge C. L. Smith, president of the Minnesota State Horticultural Society, reviewed the gains that had been made. Much had been accomplished, he said. The native thick-skinned puckering plum had been replaced with numerous improvements; the Wealthy was "one of the ten best commercial apples in America."[425] But there was more to be done.

Late in the twentieth century, horticulturists might issue the same challenge. Minnesota's climate still poses problems and growers have much work to do. Nevertheless, thanks to the efforts of gardeners who have gone before them, modern gardeners have roses, azaleas, fruit and shade trees of all kinds. Their cottages, as Judge Smith said, are "nestled amongst maples, elms, and pine," their yards "made beautiful with the rose, the peony, the iris, the hollyhock, and the golden glow."[426]

•—◆—•

On any Saturday during the growing season, local farmers' markets double as florists and nurseries.

Winona limestone surrounds the water-lily pond at Squire House Gardens, an English country garden and shop in Afton.

Lynn Steiner

GARDENING

RENAISSANCE

1970 - 1995

·—◆—·

*Many of the old-fashioned perennials in the front yard
of the Michael Anderson family home in Stillwater
have been growing there for a century.*

IDEAS FROM ABROAD

Walk down any street in Central London . . . or along any country lane and you are overwhelmed by flowers. Flowers in gardens and in the fields, flowers in pots and other containers, flowers in windowboxes on the second floor. . . . There are flowers growing out of a bit of soil by a corner of a building, [and] out of a crack in the concrete.

Peter Olin, writing from England, 1994.[427]

The late twentieth century has witnessed a tremendous increase in gardens and gardening. By the 1990s gardening had become America's most popular leisure activity; one in three adults participated in some form: indoor plants, vegetables, perennial borders, landscape design, heirloom plants, and community plots, among others. These interests have translated into results the whole community can enjoy.

Annuals have augmented evergreens around businesses and institutions. Museums have added gardens to their collections; vacant lots have become thriving vegetable and flower plots. Flowers have sprouted in front yards and jumped city sidewalks to bloom on boulevards.

Garden plots and designs are as varied as the individuals and groups who plant them. Specialty gardeners, such as rose fanciers, lily growers, and dahlia experts, can be found in every neighborhood. Carpet bedding is alive and thriving at parks and institutions; Central Park in Roseville, for example, has six hundred linear feet of flowers "bedded out." Terraced estate gardens near Lake Minnetonka and White Bear grow lovelier every year. In fact, gardening styles persist from decade to decade, never completely gone even when others are in vogue.

Interest in landscape architecture has grown considerably in recent years. One of the most eloquent and talented landscape architects is Herb Baldwin of Jordan, Minnesota, designer of estate and institutional gardens, former teacher at the University of Minnesota, and mentor to many. Now called the "grandfather" of landscape architecture in Minnesota, Baldwin has been at the forefront for decades. His designs are elegant and natural looking; if pressed, he will say that his work is linked more with England's garden tradition than any other. But in designing a garden, he is most interested in "the quality of space."[428]

Fred and Alice Wall used a French country approach in the garden around their Wayzata home.

Visitors to Jo Ryo En (The Garden of Quiet Listening) at Carlton College in Northfield are encouraged to pause in the Viewing Pavilion.

·—◆—·

Amateurs and professionals alike have been influenced by many ideas and styles. No one trend dominates, but at least three influences are evident in today's gardens: *inspiration from abroad, inspiration from the past,* and *ideas from nature.* Interestingly, these same influences have been seen in Minnesota gardens throughout the state's history.

The first Minnesotans were scarcely conscious of looking abroad for garden inspiration. Their situations were too rough and time constraints too great to allow for much reflection. But even at an early date they borrowed from other cultures. Many of the earliest hired gardeners were immigrants, often German or Scandinavian, trained in the traditions of the homeland. No doubt, they brought aspects of their training to their work in Minnesota.

In 1857 the *St. Paul Daily Pioneer and Democrat* wrote of Dr. Alfred E. Ames's garden: "[It was] arranged by the fine taste of the German man who superintends the garden."[429] Occasionally immigrants of means, like August Schell in New Ulm, worked to re-create the landscapes they had left behind.

Somewhat later, people like Frederick Nussbaumer, who had worked at the great gardens of Europe, began gardening in parks and private estates. Their vision was a key factor in bringing fine gardens to Minnesota.

By the end of the nineteenth century, many wealthy citizens had traveled to Europe, England, and the Orient and were inspired to reproduce aspects of the gardens they had visited. Italy was admired and emulated for its sculpture and terraces; England for its perennial borders, rock gardens, and public parks. The topiary, formal allées, and parterres of France were much sought-after. The Japanese garden, "as ancient [as those of Italy and England] but not as well known," according to businessman F. F. Fletcher of Minneapolis, was an object of fascination.[430]

International gardens have continued to intrigue Minnesotans; their sheer abundance in other countries is especially impressive to some. For others, the elegance of a particular garden is not to be forgotten. Having seen an exotic landscape, they are compelled to translate that beauty and significance to Minnesota ground.

That was true for Dr. Bardwell Smith, professor of Asian Studies at Carleton College in Northfield. On his first visit to Japan in 1965, Dr. Smith was struck "by the beauty and the antiquity"[431] of gardens in Kyoto and determined then to create something similar at his home campus. Because the college's involvement with Asia had been long and fruitful, his plans for a garden were met with great enthusiasm.

After Dr. Smith had made several attempts to locate a designer, a visiting professor from Kyoto suggested that he contact David Slawson, a young landscape architect from Cleveland, Ohio. Slawson had studied for two years under Kinsaku Nakane, one of Japan's finest designers. Although he had a doctorate in Japanese Aesthetics and Literature, Slawson was still a relatively untried artist whose work had been limited to a few gardens. The choice was a felicitous one: Slawson not only designed a fine garden for Carleton, but has become nationally known for his work. He is the author of *The Secret Teachings in the Art of the Japanese Garden.*[432]

Between 1974 and 1976 Slawson designed and constructed the $15,000 garden, which was financed by foundation grants and people interested in the project. By the fall of 1976 "Jo Ryo En" (The Garden of Quiet Listening) was completed. In speaking of its design, Nakane told Slawson: "You have completely grasped the beauty of the Japanese garden and made it your own."[433]

The garden is a Kare-sansui, or dry landscape garden. The presence of water is suggested by a band of smooth, gray stones and a lake-like configuration of white gravel. Jo Ryo En is intended for meditation, not for strolling through, and visitors are invited to pause at several vantage points along a stepping-stone path. Framed within the hedges and surrounding shrubbery are two stone lanterns, mounds of evergreens, small trees, and ground covers of various kinds. The lichen-covered rocks were all collected by Slawson and the Smiths within a one hundred-mile radius of Northfield. The garden is a masterful arrangement of shapes and colors, inviting the visitor to absorb its beauty. Western eyes may not understand the subtleties behind the placement of rocks and other objects in the garden, but they can appreciate the cool grays and greens of plants and stones and the gentle blending of soft and hard surfaces.

"The name represents fairly accurately how the garden is used," explained Dr. Smith. "We waited to see how people would relate to the space before we named it. People sit here alone or in small groups and listen quietly. They say it represents a respite from a busy life."[434]

Gardeners in Bloomington helped to create a respite from a busy life as well, when they planned and financed the Normandale Japanese Garden. Their motivation, though, came not from a visit to the Orient, but a desire to make a contribution to the community.

In 1964 Bloomington was boom country. Farmland was being turned into suburban lots, and several parks were under construction. "And there were no trees," said garden club member Pat Barger.[435] Enter the Bloomington Affiliated Garden Clubs which planted 35,000 trees in city school grounds and parks. The Sears Foundation awarded the group five hundred dollars for its efforts. "We wanted to give something back to the community," said club member Yvonne Bublitz.[436]

"After looking at several options, we decided to build a Japanese garden because of its uniqueness," explained Yvonne, co-chair with Evia "Bunny" Aaze of the initial Japanese garden committee. "There really was not another one in the state at that time. We knew this would be very educational."[437] Their choice of site also affected the garden type.

The Normandale campus, still being developed, had a wonderful lake known as Green Heron Pond.[438] Garden club members asked for a two-acre piece of college property, including a portion of the pond; they would raise the estimated $75,000 needed for the project, and the college would maintain the site. "We wanted this to be a place where people could experience nature," said Pat Barger.[439]

From the beginning, the group had widespread support from the community. "We estimated that we got a $500,000 garden for $100,000," said Pat, "because so much was donated." Takao Watanabe, landscape architect for the Tokyo Metropolitan Government, designed the garden and supervised its construction. "He dedicated extensive time over the years to the project," explained Pat, "and continues to check on the site periodically."

The sand and fill were donated, and the drivers volunteered their time and trucks. Workers from Minneapolis brought clay excavated from city construction sites. Nurseries gave plant material. "We were fortunate to have so much help," said Yvonne Bublitz. "Everyone, from Dr. Leon Snyder who advised us, to the college who gave the land and has maintained the garden, helped us make the project a success."[440]

Assistance also came from Japanese-Americans who wanted to express their thanks for the welcome extended to them during World War II. Japanese-American veterans of the military intelligence service language school, who had been stationed at Camp Savage and Fort Snelling during the war, gave $25,000 for two structures: the Bentendo, a hexagonal-shaped building implying good fortune, and the Taiko-bashi, a drum-shaped bridge. Through the years local Japanese-Americans have continued their support, serving on the garden committee and helping to plan and serve the annual Sukiyaki fund-raising dinner.

Called a Japanese hill garden, the site was dedicated in 1976. Walking through the space, visitors encounter water in various wonderful forms. The garden is built around the perimeter of a good-sized pond, where to one side, a waterfall empties into a small stream. In the distance is a marshy lake. Bridges cross the water in several places, giving visitors the chance to experience the landscape from different vantage points.

Tranquil shades of green predominate, but colorful blooms and bright foliage are used when appropriate. In spring visitors can see the flowers of snowmound spirea, red splendor crab, and azalea mollis, followed by the Japanese tree lilac in June and the peegee hydrangea in August. In fall, winged euonymus, purple leaf sand cherry, and sugar maple add a fiery splendor to the cool greens. The garden wears well in winter: clear silhouettes, large evergreens, and colorful bark are elegant against the snow.

The garden has been all the planners hoped for. "It is so restful, a place for refreshment of the spirit . . . and a quiet retreat from a busy, urban life," said Bublitz.[441]

In designing her St. Paul garden in the 1980s, Vera Trent also looked abroad, turning to England for two reasons. "Our home is an English country cottage, and I believe in relating the garden to the house," she explained. More importantly, "I'm a romantic. I like the wild look."[442]

Trent's front yard stands apart from the closely-clipped lawns along her block. From the boulevard to the front door, there are flowers—one hundred fifty different varieties of perennials in bloom from May to October. Early spring brings pansies, tulips, trilliums, lilacs, and several kinds of wild geraniums. In June there are roses of various sorts, false indigo, iris, Oriental poppies, and lupines. In high summer she has daisies, liatris, lilies, and phlox. The season closes with several hues of asters and chrysanthemums. To be in her garden is to stand waist-deep in blossoms.

Trent started modestly with only one border in the front. At the time, she "didn't know a rose from a radish. Every year I would dig up a little more lawn." She learned about gardening by reading and by doing—"You can't make mistakes in the garden."

·—◆—·

Vera Trent's cottage garden in St. Paul is ablaze with color all season.

Northland Arboretum, Ron Morriem

The garden is Vera's, but husband Jim has added some wonderful improvements. Several years ago, he built an elegant wrought-iron fence, which not only defines the space, but looks as though it has been there fifty years. Since, he has installed a seven-sided bird bath set on granite, and brick paths. The walks are not only beautiful—aged brick interlaced with granite—but functional. "Before he put in the paths," said Vera, "I had trouble working in many parts of the garden. Now I can reach all the flowers."

In Vera's garden, fragrance is as important as hue. After the lilacs, there are peonies and roses, followed by oregano, lavender, hyssop, and a variety of mints and thymes. Milkweed has seeded itself, adding to the general loveliness. Phlox, roses, and Russian sage lean against the gate. "It's wonderful to have the sage there," Vera said. "As people come in, they brush against it."

Despite the very settled look of the garden, Vera maintains, "I'm really just a beginning gardener. There are many other ideas I'd like to try."

Walking in John and Sheila Stollers' Minneapolis garden is akin to being in the back yard of an English town house. The similarity is no accident. On his city lot, John Stoller has worked to create a reminder of home for his wife Sheila. "My wife is English," said John. "I wanted to create this environment for her that is a reflection of an English landscape."[443]

Tall, trellis-topped fences and lush plantings enclose the space. Clematis and bittersweet clamber over the fences; a tapestry of small trees and shrubs grows against them. Crowded in front are ferns, grasses, ground covers, and perennials of all sorts.

Stoller chooses plants as much for their foliage, shape, and texture as for their bloom. The dark, rough leaves of Japanese anemone contrast with the silky, grey-green hosta, and both are set off by spikey, perennial blue salvia. In another bed, lacy moonbeam coreopsis stands shoulder to shoulder with perennial geraniums.

"I like a sense of order and formality, but within that, a sense of exuberance." A strong design and meticulously kept grass and beds provide the order; lush plantings give spontaneity.

Gardeners make the best use of exotic models when they are inspired to create the "feel of the place," as Stoller did, rather than a literal replication. Volunteers at the Northland Arboretum in Brainerd had a similar experience in developing a wildlife area and wildflower trail near Whisky Creek.

Director Richard Beal, who had long admired French

Impressionist Claude Monet, shared the book *Monet's Passion* with master gardener Janice Bradshaw. "The author gave diagrams of Monet's garden and his flowers," recalled Bradshaw. "We were looking at the pictures of Giverny and the charts, and it was very inspiring. We both looked at each other and said, 'We can do that.'"[444]

And do it they have. Janice began by drawing up a list of wildflowers that could survive in northern Minnesota and still match the colors Monet used. "We planted for wildlife as well as beauty," she explained. Many of the plants came from volunteer Prudence Query, who grows wildflowers in her home greenhouses. "Pru was very knowledgeable and very enthusiastic about wildflowers," said Janice.[445] In addition, volunteers kept an eye out for undeveloped lands about to be bulldozed and rescued plants.

Planting began in 1992; the next year volunteers doubled the area's size. They doubled it again in 1994, planting wildflowers along two thousand feet of trails around the pond.[446] In spring hikers might see the blue-violet anemone, Jack-in-the-pulpit, pale bloodroot, or rosy prairie phlox along the paths. Bright yellow marsh marigolds and blue flag light up the pond.

By midsummer the blues and pinks of purple coneflower, harebell, prairie clover, blue vervain, blazing star, and yarrow are scattered along the trail. Fall brings flaming-red cardinal flower, goldenrods, and pastel-colored asters.

When workers added a Monet-esque bridge in 1993, "that really brought the whole look together," said Janice.[447]

The bridge differs from Monet's in one important respect—it's handicapped accessible. To get the right design, Beal took every book he had on Monet to the Continental Bridge Company of Alexandria, Minnesota. "I told them we wanted the look and the color, but it had to meet the new accessibility laws," Beal explained.[448] On a misty morning, the curved green bridge, the elegant water lilies, and tall pastel flowers make the area a convincing imitation of its French model.

Beal has worked to establish ties with the Monet Foundation in France. For the present, the two institutions have agreed to exchange ideas and products. "We carry some of the Giverny items in our gift shop; in turn they handle ours."[449] An American artist who paints at Giverny is coming to Brainerd to paint the Minnesota Monet landscape.

"It's been exciting to watch this landscape develop," said Janice.[450] The arboretum has even added a little green boat, "except ours is a green canoe," said Beal. "Monet with a Minnesota twist."[451]

"The arboretum is beautiful," added Bradshaw, "but this is not an exact duplication of Giverny; it's just an impression."[452]

GRANDMOTHER'S GARDEN

The old fashioned garden! What a host of memories come sweeping back. . . .
What a riot of color wherever we looked—over towards the fence a thicket of sky
blue delphiniums whence comes the incessant hum of bees; against the grape arbor
the first hollyhocks just unfolding their pink and white rosettes.

Northrup King Sterling Seed Catalogue, 1915.[453]

Looking to the past for garden inspiration is not unique to late-twentieth century Minnesotans. Even the Victorians cast their sights wistfully to earlier times. In 1899 Charlotte O. Van Cleve remembered a time "many years ago" when "morning glories ran riot over our fences" and "children hurrying to school, stopped a moment to look at and admire the many hued beauty."[454] That same year Mrs. A. A. Kennedy of Hutchinson recalled her mother's garden when the "old-fashioned flowers . . . far excelled the flowers of today."[455]

These gardeners were reacting to carpet-bedding, in which masses of gaudily colored annuals were planted in stylized arrangements, displacing hardy perennial and biennial flowers. Lost along with these simple flowers, said Charlotte, was the simple life of "mother's teaching and father's prayer."[456]

In Mankato, grounds around the 1871 Hubbard House
are lovingly maintained by volunteers.

Seventeen years later, writers were still applauding the old-fashioned garden. *The Minnesotan* magazine in 1916 described in great detail how to achieve the "garden your grandmother set out," which, said the author, was once again popular.[457] Recommended plants were lupines, foxgloves, larkspur, peonies, phlox, iris, and hollyhocks with rue and baby's breath for "soft, misty effects among the border."[458]

Northrup King seed catalogues offered pages of hardy plants for "the dear old place where we joyfully tripped after our grandmother as she pottered about." Gardeners could buy a "grandmother's collection" of Canterbury bells, cup and saucer, shasta daisy, coreopsis, delphiniums, gaillardia, and hollyhocks. In this garden, said the writer, even the swallows seem "peaceful and happy."[459]

The invitation to old-style gardens has been heard repeatedly throughout Minnesota's history, most recently in our own era. The turmoil and social upheaval of the late 1960s onward led many to question our pell-mell rush toward industrialization, and Minnesotans looked back, just as Van Cleve had done, on a simple life of "mother's teaching . . . father's prayer."

Old houses, country furniture, and vintage clothes took on new appeal. Young families headed "back to the land" to recover the traditions and beauty they remembered. Individuals undertook the arduous task of renovating dilapidated Victorian houses. In saving the house, many felt, they were rescuing the neighborhood.

On the gardening front, they discovered styles that had been pushed aside in the 1950s and '60s in favor of bright rows of annuals and lines of evergreens. Herb plots, knot gardens, hardy perennials, and old-fashioned roses began to reappear, appropriate framing for historic buildings. Features that had disappeared with the advent of the patio—trellises, benches, ponds, and arbors—once more became standard items in the garden.

For many modern gardeners, their historic homes demand vintage landscaping. Bea and Larry Westerberg, who bought a 1905 farmhouse outside of Hastings, sensed that planting perennial flowers and heirloom varieties of vegetables and fruits was "the right thing to do," said Bea. "It's really interesting to think that we might be raising plants that grew here when our house was new."[460]

From their house on a hill, the Westerbergs and daughter Nissa look out over a landscape from an earlier time. Flowers line the driveway, spill out of window boxes, and blanket the lawn. An apple orchard with many antique varieties, in addition to plums, apricots, and pears, can be found out back. An herb patch, with plants varying from angelica to verbena, provides seasoning for meals and materials for potpourri and dyeing. An enormous vegetable plot stretches behind the house. Among the hundreds of vegetables are forty-two varieties of potatoes and numerous tomatoes, including Anna Russian, green grape, and Amana orange, all varieties the settlers could have grown.

Many of the names of their plants have a time-honored ring. "Improved King Phillip" was one of the first corns grown in Minnesota. A melon variety from 1889, "so old they thought it was lost for a while," said Bea, is called "Moon and Stars," [461] named for the bright yellow dots and crescents on its dark green skin.

For the Westerbergs, finding heirloom and unusual varieties is half the fun. Larry and a friend, Howard Krosch of Stillwater, like exploring old or abandoned orchards for scion wood that can be used for grafting. Some of the apples they have found—Transcendent, Wedge, Folwell, and Geneva—might have grown in pioneer John Harris's orchard.

To facilitate their collection of the rare and intriguing, the Westerbergs joined Seed Savers Exchange in Decorah, Iowa. The organization stores seeds that are no longer commercially produced (sixteen thousand varieties in the mid-1990s) and coordinates

exchanges between members. Each year it publishes a directory with several hundred pages of available seeds. In it, the Westerbergs list seeds they are willing to trade and select others they would like to try.

The Westerbergs' lifestyle is certainly not a leisurely one. In addition to their regular jobs, they have the enormous task of keeping up the gardens and selling their produce at the Hastings Farmers Market on Saturdays. They make their own beer and wine, prepare jams and jellies, dry flowers, and make wreaths. But they wouldn't consider giving it up. "There are always more plants we'd like to try," explained Larry.[462] Besides, added Bea, "it's a way of touching our heritage."[463]

Today's public re-creations are another way to step back in time. Minnesotans can slip into the spirit of the past at various places around the state. In historic Forestville State Park, south of Rochester, cosmos and delphinium bloom beside a clapboard Victorian house. Out back, a vegetable patch matches one that might have prospered at the turn of the century.

At the Olmsted County History Center in Rochester, the Heritage Garden contains herbs, flowers, and vegetables a typical prairie pioneer family might have grown. To assure authenticity, master gardener Lou Hoppa uses seeds from the Cornell University agriculture department, which serves as a clearing-house for information on traditional American gardens.[464]

To sample the Twin Cities of the 1850s, visitors can stop at the Ard Godfrey House at Chute Square or the John Stevens house in Minnehaha Park, both built within a year of each other in Minneapolis. The Godfrey house was the first home on the east side of the Mississippi River; Stevens was the first on the river's west bank.

The Greek Revival Godfrey house at University and Central Avenues is in the heart of industrial Minneapolis. Once past the split-rail fence covered with wild clematis and grape vines, the visitor gets a sense of the simple beauty of early Minnesota homes.

Ard Godfrey was brought here from Maine by early entrepreneur Franklin Steele to build a sawmill at St. Anthony Falls. As part of his contract, Steele promised a suitable dwelling for the Godfrey family. Built in 1849 near the river, the frame building was home to Ard, his wife Harriet, and their children for five years.[465]

In the 1970s the Minneapolis Woman's Club meticulously restored the house and furnishings, even reproducing the wallpaper from a fragment of the original. For the grounds, the club sought help from Mary Maguire Lerman, horticulturist with the

Minneapolis Park Board. Using historic photographs, the Godfreys' letters, old nursery catalogues, and lists of native plants, Lerman devised a plan for the yard. It called for old-fashioned roses and common lilacs, lots of prairie plants (swamp milkweed, butterfly weed, prairie smoke, and goldenrod), and a small herb plot by the kitchen door. "We used native herbs, like giant hyssop, wild onion and garlic from the prairie—plants they would have been able to find," Lerman explained.[466]

Dandelions grow in profusion about the yard; it seems that Harriet Godfrey missed the tender greens from back East and asked that they be sent to her place in Minnesota.

"The small house and garden are a hidden treasure," said Lerman. "You really get an idea of what early settlers had to deal with."

To experience the best of what Victorians might have enjoyed, visitors can stop at the Palmer Centennial Place in Mankato. There, by the Hubbard House, home to the Blue Earth County Museum, is a re-created turn-of-the-century park.

In 1871 R. D. Hubbard, co-founder of Hubbard Milling Company, built his family home at the corner of South Broad and Warren Streets. Nearly a century later the Hubbards

D.R. Martin

Restoring historic architecture often leads to vintage gardens, such as this one of Sarah Kinney in St. Paul.

deeded their home to Blue Earth County for its museum. Hubbard Milling, to celebrate its centennial in 1978, gave the city a formal landscaped park adjacent to the house.[467] In consultation with Minneapolis architect Foster Dunwiddie, landscape architects from the Jordan, Minnesota, firm of Charles Wood Associates researched gardens, parks, and plant varieties that might have existed when the Hubbards lived there.

The resulting garden—flowers in parterres, an arbor, a sunken "outdoor room," herb gardens, and elegant stonework—shows the Victorian period at its grandest. Long perennial beds anchored with peonies, daylilies, and iris add color from spring to fall. The shrubs, including common lilac, coxspur hawthorne, arrow-head viburnum, alpine currant, and spirea, might have been grown on the Hubbard family lawn. Light fixtures, recast from the same molds used in 1900, add to the feel of authenticity.

The Hubbard House itself was restored in 1994, enabling visitors to savor the home and garden together. Since its inception, the garden has been lovingly maintained by the Twilight Garden Club. "It's always easy to get volunteers," said garden club member Marcia Qualset, "because the garden is so beautiful. Many people go out of their way to walk by and tell us how wonderful everything looks."[468]

Sometimes gardeners don't turn to the past; rather, the past keeps resurfacing. Involving children in the garden is one concept that waxes and wanes with the decades. Each time it reappears, gardening is viewed as a solution to the era's social problems. Pioneers expected their children and every other able-bodied member of the household to plant, weed, and water. Victorians believed that gardening was a civilizing activity for the young. Caring for tender plants was said to encourage gentleness and was a painless way to offer sex education.

In the early twentieth century, school gardens were thought to edify and properly direct young minds away from city temptations. Again during the Depression, young people were urged to garden, both to produce food for the family and to beautify the homestead. But after World War II and the all-involving efforts of the Victory gardens, children seem to have been left out of the garden for a time.

Over the past two decades, adults have once more invited children to cultivate their own gardens. Their aims this time have been to nurture self-esteem, to encourage cooperation, and to teach environmental awareness. Organizers also hope children will learn where food comes from. "Gardening is more important now than ever," said Sandy Tanck, director of youth programming at the Minnesota Landscape Arboretum, "because in their growing up,

most children are removed from the close relationship with plants that our ancestors had."[469]

Commercial and non-profit institutions have made great efforts to encourage young gardeners. Seed companies package and sell easy-to-grow flowers and vegetables; publishers produce brightly colored how-to books for young gardeners. Garden centers set aside areas of their stores for youngsters, complete with small tools, gardening gloves, and hats. Nature centers, playgrounds, and arboretums conduct gardening programs that range from morning workshops to summer-long camps.

Gardens like the one at the Children's Museum in St. Paul, are designed to appeal to the young. Children can view an alphabet of plants, ageratum to zinnia, or walk through a Bean Pole Promenade in the vegetable patch. They can learn about weather or explore plants in the Scensorium where plants are selected for their fragrance and texture.

Adults who help children in the garden attest to the power of plants and the joys of working in the soil. Tim Kenny, an instructor with the Minnesota Landscape Arboretum has seen more than one "small miracle." At one of the arboretum's inner-city gardens, each five- by five-foot plot is worked by a team of two children. "The first day a brother and sister came in. Their mother thought it would be a good idea for the siblings to share a plot," Kenny explained.[470] "They didn't like the idea at all. Their arms were crossed, their expressions firm, they were having none of it."

As a last-ditch measure, Kenny put a string exactly down the middle and said each child could garden on his own side of the string. "About four weeks into the project," said Kenny, "the sister came and said she had something to show me. I tried to handle her question on the spot, but she insisted that I come see. When I got to their plot, the brother and sister each took hold of one end of the string, pulled it up and threw it away, making one garden. For the rest of the summer, they worked together, harvested together, and at least in the garden, got along."

Community gardening can work minor miracles. Every twenty or thirty years, towns and neighborhoods rediscover its benefits. Under the banners of patriotism, work relief, city beautification, or wholesome food production, gardens can improve morale and sustain the community.

In the 1970s the rise of environmental awareness inspired many to return to the soil. An uncertain economy added financial motivation. People of all ages and abilities began to convert vacant lots into productive vegetable gardens. In the process they came to know their neighbors and developed community-building skills.

Soon, gardeners applied what they learned to other projects, like planting trees along streets stripped bare by Dutch elm disease and growing flowers on Main Street. Dauntless in the face of significant obstacles, many have tackled enormous projects.

A group in St. Paul, led by Bonnie Lawrence of the Merriam Park Environmental Committee, landscaped a mile-long section of embankment along the I-94 freeway. To insure success, Lawrence and the committee recruited workers, arranged for refreshments, borrowed tools, interested the media, and organized planting.[471]

On a wet, cold Saturday in April 1993, over two hundred volunteers in orange safety vests spread out across the sloping roadside, shovels and plants in hand. That day they planted seventeen hundred shrubs and trees provided by the Minnesota Department of Transportation; a month later they added twenty-five hundred wildflowers.

By any measure, the project was a success. "People had a good time doing it, and the benefits will be there for years to come," said Lawrence. "We were able to accomplish a $50,000 project for $4,000." When asked how she is able to tackle so much, Lawrence said she never believes people who say that something can't be done. "You hear enough about the terrible things wrong with the world," she said. "I want to show that you can start to turn things around."

Volunteers in Silver Bay had their own hand at "turning things around," designing a project to capture the imagination of their community. Silver Bay, a mining town on the shore of Lake Superior, was known more for taconite than scenic beauty. After 1986, when Reserve Mining Company declared bankruptcy and moved out, the town experienced recession and dwindling population.[472]

In 1988 city planner Duane Northagen and four volunteers—Pat Reed, Betty Hylden, Arlene Bjella, and Steve Meyer—started a landscaping project that would involve young people and spur community pride. Their idea: a Marigold Trail leading from Highway 61 to the heart of town. "We wanted something that the little kids could get excited about," said Reed.[473]

In April 1989 the committee helped 350 elementary school children plant and nurture marigolds in ice cream cups. "Every child planted a seed," Pat said, "enough to blanket 1,100 linear feet of Outer Drive."[474]

That May the students were bussed to Outer Drive to plant their small flowers. "The kids got so excited and proud," said Reed. "They all knew exactly where their marigold was and brought their parents out later to look."[475]

The flower trail was only the first of several landscape improvements, including one hundred new trees along Outer Drive, a new Silver Bay entrance sign, flower-lined nature trails near the Minnesota Veterans Home, a rock garden in front of city hall, and flower boxes and gardens in town. A youth group, Kids Plus, maintains the landscaping on Outer Drive. And every year, Marigold Trail is replanted.

"This has been the most gratifying thing I've ever done," said Reed. "People stop and tell us how wonderful it looks. 'You've made a real difference in the town,' they say. In fact, other communities now use us as an example for their own projects."[476]

Duane Northagen

"We've seen substantial improvement in the downtown area," added Duane Northagen. "Stores are remodeling. Sidewalks have been redone and parking lots improved. We give credit to the Outer Drive project."[477] The dedicated volunteers in Silver Bay had rediscovered an old lesson: in nurturing a garden, they nurtured a community.

WORKING
WITH NATURE

We often seem to place a greater value on plants imported from other countries than what we place on our native species. In my travels I have noticed that, for instance, Australians feature plants that are native to Europe and America. While in southern California, more Australian plants are used than one would see in gardens in Sydney or Melbourne.

Dr. Leon Snyder, *Native Plants for Northern Gardens.* [478]

From the first, Minnesotans have had a love affair with nature. Nineteenth-century writers sang the praises of the wild things, listing the flowers, shrubs, and trees they found here. Throughout its 100-plus-year history, the *Minnesota Horticulturist* featured voices lauding the state's rich flora. Charlotte Van Cleve, for example, who could always be counted on for sensible commentary on things horticultural, spoke in 1887 about "Wild Flowers." For many years she had been convinced that

we should take more notice than we do of the wild flowers so lavishly scattered over our prairies and woodlands, and that we might with great pleasure and profit domesticate them in our lawns and flowerbeds. They are hardy and, once planted, would come up year by year and amply reward our care with their rich, bright colors and graceful foliage.[479]

Almost from the beginning, a tone of lament can be heard whenever writers speak of indigenous flora. In 1910 Lycurgus Rose Moyer, prominent Montevideo citizen and banker and a well-known botanist, read a paper before the Minnesota Academy of Science. Speaking of land along the upper Minnesota River, he noted that

. . . the showey [sic] prairie flowers are gone, and even the grasses have been mostly destroyed. Along the roadsides and on railroad rights-of-way a few individuals of the original flora are still to be found.[480]

Cindie Sinclair of Camrose Hill, a flower farm near Stillwater, finds inspiration for her floral designs in the nearby woods and fields.

Two years later Professor Dietrich Lange of St. Paul, educator, author, and director of nature studies for the St. Paul schools, wrote with a note of urgency: "Pieces of land from a quarter section to one or more sections should be set aside as wild plant reserves. Unless that is done soon, the coming generations can never know how the country looked in which their fathers made their homes."[481]

Preservation of wildlife remained a continuing concern throughout the century. Eloise Butler's Wild Botanic Garden was one person's remarkable response to the problem. Garden clubs as well urged respect for indigenous plants and animals. Protection of wildflowers, and by extension, all the state's natural beauty, was a mission of the Minnesota Garden Flower Society. In 1923 the group explained the reason for their work—"The ax of man . . . has cleared the way [and] destroyed much of this beauty—partly through necessity and partly through thoughtlessness."[482]

Long before native plants were popular additions to gardens, May Wright, the late grande dame of Minnesota flora, collected seeds, propagated plants, and spoke and wrote passionately about Minnesota's vast wild treasure. Her White Bear property with its extensive woodland gardens was a popular stopping place of garden tours from the 1960s until her death in 1995.

Beginning in 1940 and continuing into the 1960s, the use of chemicals was highly touted in the media and advertisements. Interest in the lawn was at its most intense, and articles in the local press urged all manner of pesticides and herbicides in the war on weeds and bugs. Information about wild flora and fauna took a secondary role.

Then in 1962 Rachel Carson's book *Silent Spring* burst upon the gardening scene. The reaction, said *Time*'s science editor, "was almost entirely favorable, and by no means [did] all the letters come from faddists and hysterical women."[483] Carson's book became a catalyst for concern about the use of chemicals and was a major factor in spurring laws that would eliminate several deadly pesticides.

By the 1970s gardeners had discovered they could improve the environment in their own yards. One response was to limit the use of chemicals. Some became devoted organic gardeners, foreswearing pesticides, herbicides, and fungicides of all kinds. They learned to apply compost and mulch, items which had been standard treatments of the 1920s and before, and to use the ladybug and praying mantis for insect control.

Other gardeners, while not becoming totally organic, adopted the principles of "integrated pest management." Under that banner, they used a variety of sensible measures to ward off trouble before it escalated.

In addition, gardeners began to look at the landscape differently. They added native trees, grasses, prairie flowers, and woodland ground covers. Many learned to landscape for wildlife, using plants that provide food or shelter for wild birds and mammals. For some, the lawn was no longer the essential feature of the yard. Homeowners extended their borders, placed ground covers beneath trees, dug ponds, and constructed arbors. The wide emerald swath had become an accent, not a focal point. By the late twentieth century, almost every neighborhood had examples of nature-friendly landscaping.

Some gardeners, like Carol Kollander of St. Paul, even had their own miniature prairie. An expert gardener, Kollander had maintained an extensive rockery, grape arbors, and woodland garden for years. Then, in the late 1980s she took a Minnesota Landscape Arboretum-sponsored tour around Lake Minnetonka. "One of the participants had put in a prairie," Carol said, "and I thought, 'Oh, that *is* pretty.' Since I had a vacant piece of property, I wanted to try one myself."[484]

With the advice of Landscape Alternatives, a Roseville nursery specializing in native plants, Kollander started her own fifty-five-foot-square tall-grass prairie. Wanting results fast, she purchased plants, not seeds. "I put the plants in rather haphazardly, with no real plan," she said.

No matter. Kollander's prairie is wonderful, a sea of color from spring to fall. Standing amid ten-foot cup-plants and shoulder-high coneflowers and black-eyed Susans, visitors forget that the city is only feet away. Birds and butterflies are fooled, too. Meadowlarks, finches, monarchs, and swallow-tailed butterflies frequent her yard.

Maintenance is minimal, although once a year Kollander must cut down all the plants, a city person's substitute for prairie wildfires. And from time to time, because her rich soil encourages rank growth, she needs to pull out some of the more aggressive varieties.

Mostly, she enjoys wandering through her prairie, adding new plants and picking flowers. "I have always loved wildflowers and I hate to mow," she said. "This has been such fun. It looks so beautiful."

•——◆——•

Carol Kollander has recreated a prairie on her city lot in St. Paul. In August the yard is bright with purple coneflowers, ox-eye daisies, and lobelia.

*Char Menzel's spring rock garden is
a blend of natives and exotics.*

· — ◆ — ·

Not all gardeners can accommodate an entire prairie, but many have added native plants of various kinds. Char Menzel of Dellwood, a master gardener since 1981, started planting Minnesota wildflowers in 1984 after a visit to May Wright's place in nearby White Bear Lake. There, she gained a new appreciation for native flora. "I was really taken with the beauty," she recalled.[485] Since then, Char has joined the Minnesota Native Plant Society and her own garden has become a training ground for others.

When Menzel began, she "just started incorporating native plants into the other gardens. I thought the spring plants, trilliums, and hepaticas, were especially beautiful and put those in first." She gradually began to refine the overgrown wild area in the back, pulling out invasive exotics, and adding trails and Minnesota varieties.

Because most of her one-acre lot in Dellwood is shady, Menzel concentrated on woodland varieties: Jeffersonia, ferns, iris, and hepaticas in combination with non-natives like pulmonarias, sweet woodruff, and Japanese aruncas. Shades of green and grey provide the background; white and pastels tint the flowers. Her gardens are a cool, peaceful evocation of the north woods.

Menzel has found, as have others who grow them, that native plants are very hardy. "One fall when we had a sudden cold snap and lots of our bulbs died, I didn't lose a single native plant," said Menzel.

"They're adapted to all of Minnesota's odd quirks." Chiefly, though, she grows native plants for their beauty. "They're lovely, and they're very subtle. I'm appreciating that more all the time."

Jim Hagstrom, owner of Savanna Designs in Lake Elmo, has been landscaping with native plants since 1973 when he was an under-graduate at the University of Minnesota. "I went to college when ecology was first popular, and I was around for the first Earth Day. Even then, other kinds of landscaping seemed unnatural to me."[486]

Hagstrom prefers native plants, largely because of his commitment to environmental awareness and sustainable landscapes. But his primary reason is aesthetic. "To me, our native indigenous landscape is more interesting and subtly beautiful than any one we could import."

Hagstrom ascribes his love for wild things to time spent with his grandfather, a tree farmer and naturalist. "I worked with him in my childhood and learned about native plants," he said. In his landscapes, Hagstrom integrates European notions of design with native plants. "People have certain expectations for the landscape, what looks good and what looks uncared for. I've spent a lot of time in Europe absorbing ideas from historic gardens." The result of his studies is expressed in his elegant, low-maintenance designs incorporating plants of Minnesota's forests and prairies.

Landscape architect Jim Hagstrom uses native plants as an alternative to high-maintenance ones. The entryway at this Dellwood home gives evidence that natives can be elegant as well as easy to grow.

Jim Hagstrom

Using native plants gives year-round interest to the garden, said Hagstrom; they change color and shape with the seasons. "It makes no sense to plan just for the summer, which is so short in Minnesota. Gardens need to look interesting in fall and winter as well."

Linnaeus Arboretum at Gustavus Adolphus College is "beautiful in all seasons," according to Dr. Charles Mason, director.[487] The site includes a number of wonderful, specialized gardens—a hosta glade, a white garden, a rose garden composed of hardy Canadian roses, and an herb garden—all designed by landscape architect Herb Baldwin and all clustered about the Interpretive Center.

But in the arboretum proper, where space was limited and they wanted to grow the greatest amount of vegetation possible, the staff planted only Minnesota natives. "We chose the three vegetation types that get along—a conifer forest, deciduous forest, and a tall-grass prairie—because we thought it would be better to plan a natural association between plants rather than an artificial one," said Mason.

In 1994 the arboretum installed a stone prairie overlook, also designed by Baldwin, which has "added a geologic dimension to the arboretum," according to Dr. Mason. "The rocks represent different geologic eras, some of them are three and one-half million years old and some show glacial scratches."

The arboretum has attracted its share of wildlife. "A snowshoe hare has moved in," said Dr. Mason. "Deer, pheasants, all manner of birds come through, and a bald eagle from the river stops by once in a while." In addition, bluebird houses have been installed and are home to several families of bluebirds.

This has been a great "private place" for students, faculty, and the community. "When people come here," said Dr. Mason, "even though they may be tightly scheduled, they try to stay as long as they can to look at the plants because it's so peaceful and beautiful."

Part of the beauty in native landscapes comes from the wildlife they attract. Most gardeners discover, as Kollander did, that butterflies and birds quickly find their property. That's not surprising, since the habitat is improved. But increasingly, gardeners are planting specifically for wildlife.

"In fact," said Bobby Jensen, nursery landscape gardener at Lyndale Garden Center, "in about twenty-five percent of the landscape jobs we handle, clients ask that at least a part of the lawn be given back to nature. More and more people are getting away from just one big lawn. They want space for birds, butterflies, and animals."[488]

Minnesotans have been helped along by Carrol Henderson's book, *Landscaping for Wildlife*. Supervisor of non-game wildlife for the Department of Natural Resources, Henderson itemizes birds, mammals, and insects in addition to their food and shelter needs. He then provides designs for various types of yards and gardens that attract wildlife.

Response to the book has been "totally beyond my expectations," said Henderson. "People tell me they've worn off the cover."[489] Not only have home gardeners found the book helpful, but public gardens like the Brainerd Arboretum and the Minnesota Zoo have used it to plan large landscape displays.

A number of reasons account for the book's widespread acceptance. "As our rural areas are changing to subdivisions, we are taking a diverse landscape and replacing it with grass, a few shrubs, and concrete," said Henderson. "By simply planting selections attractive to wildlife, we are adding back some diversity. Even people with a tiny piece of property can grow plants to feed and shelter wildlife. And by adding features of natural beauty, we improve property values."

Landscaping for wildlife provides more than financial rewards. "The excitement starts when you put in a cardinal flower," said Henderson, "and later you look out and see a ruby-throated hummingbird sipping nectar. Then you say, 'I did it,' and you're hooked."

Nancy Gibson had just such an experience. The naturalist for the Emmy-Award-winning program *Newton's Apple*, Gibson had attempted to grow vegetables at her new home in St. Louis Park. But her lot proved too shady, so in 1989 Gibson and her family planted a butterfly garden. "We used the lists of plants attractive to butterflies as itemized in Henderson's book and put in a large border, including wild phlox, columbine, gayfeather, and globe thistle, plus trumpet vine along the fence."[490] In addition, they added berries for the birds.

The garden is successful beyond the family's expectations. "Each year we see different types of birds and butterflies," Nancy Gibson said. "That makes it exciting; you never know what you're going to get." Over the course of several summers, they've watched monarchs, eastern-tailed blue butterflies, red admirals, and tiger swallowtails, to name a few. Their son, according to Nancy, has "observed the butterflies develop from caterpillar to chrysalis to adult, and now he watches 'his' butterflies in the backyard."

Gibson's experience illustrates the guiding principle of Carrol Henderson's work: that native plants and landscape designs for wildlife are of potentially limitless interest. "What I see is their increasing utilization and promotion by landscape architects and garden centers," he said. "The enjoyment for gardeners comes not only from the beauty of the garden itself, but the extra satisfaction of watching cedar waxwings on a mountain ash or a monarch on blazing star."[491]

D.R. Martin

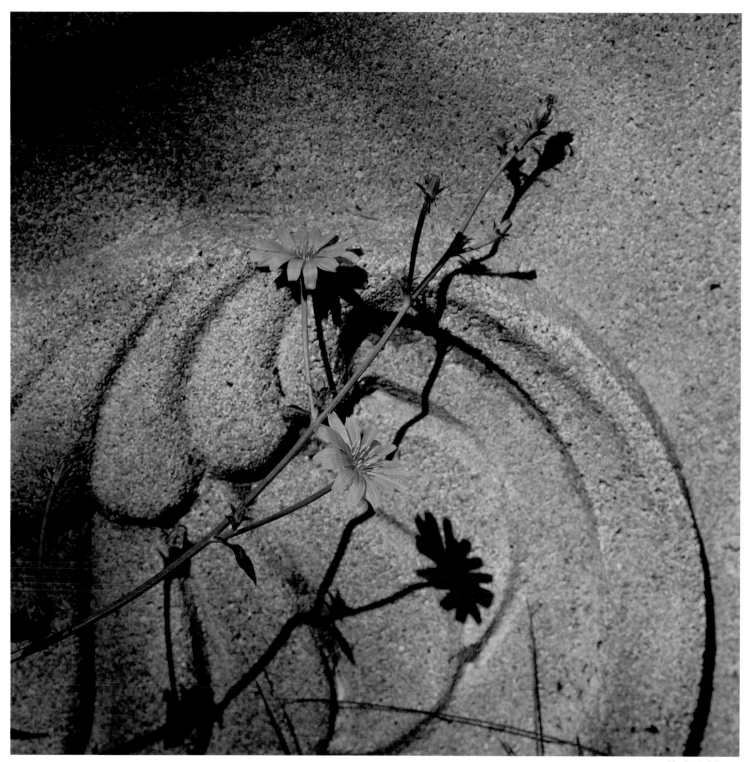

Charles J. Johnston

EPILOGUE

Every spring, untold numbers of new gardens are planted in Minnesota. All will bring some degree of joy and appreciation to their creators, whether professionals or novices, and each will, in some way, reflect the maker's desire to reconnect with the earth and its beauty.

Many of these new gardens will be shaped by impulse, like the decision of what to do with the gift of a plant from a friend. Some will replicate certain historical styles or reflect the owner's impressions of distant lands. Others will be research plots for back-yard horticulturists, diligently trying to cope with the caprices of nature.

The idea for a garden might grow from a fanciful notion, a fragrance or a shadow, the words from a poem or song. Some gardens reflect the roll of the ground or the color of the sky, or serve to complement the grace and serenity of an old piece of sculpture. The garden might simply be the fragmentary anticipation of what isn't there now, but is there by way of our inner vision.

Some of our new gardens will successfully blend aesthetic, productive, and symbolic qualities to touch the body, mind, and spirit. They will endure to enrich us again and again until, without care, they give way to a memory or become the genesis of yet another garden.

Perhaps some future gardeners will approach their projects as I do mine—thinking not only of how it will be used, but its value as a natural site. I look for a simple theme, around which I can choreograph a physical and visual symbol that will last beyond the "garden experience," etching itself in memory. My approach is suggested by the remnants of old orchard gardens in which the vacant spaces are as real as the trees left standing. These gardens-of-the-past are symbols of what I need to know in order to preserve, to renew, and to reform; they offer me a glimpse of how well I am keeping faith with nature.

In Minnesota, where the seasons demand change and variety, gardens can be bold yet gentle, big as the prairie horizon or small as a window box. Nature prescribes rigorous conditions here, but the potential expressions are unlimited. The future of the art of gardening in this state will be determined by those who embrace the idea of a garden that reflects a thriving native environment—a beautiful, bountiful place that moves the spirit.

Herb Baldwin
Landscape Architect
Jordan, Minnesota

1. Giddens, "Impressions of Minnesota," 224.
2. Bost, *A Frontier Family*, 166.
3. Davis, "Frontier Home Remedies," 369.
4. Ibid, 370.
5. Langdon, *Pioneer Gardens*, 36.
6. Farmer Seed Company Catalogue. 1898, 60.
7. Rexford, *101 Useful Weeds and Wildlings*, 10.
8. Ibid., 12, 14.
9. Jeffrey, *Frontier Women of the Trans-Mississippi West*, 73.
10. Polasek, *A Bohemian girl*, 80.
11. Drache, *The Challenge of the Prairie*, 102.
12. Dick, *Sod House Frontier*, 114.
13. Pickett, "A Pioneer Family," 309.
14. Burris, *Frontier Homes*, 61.
15. Guttersen, *Souvenir Norse-American Women*, 31.
16. Van Ravenswaay, *A 19th-Century Garden*, 20.
17. Minnesota State Horticultural Society, *Annual Report*, "History of Horticulture in Minnesota," 1873, 112. All later references to the State Horticultural Society will be abbreviated MSHS.
18. Bost, 208.
19. *Minnesota Farmer and Gardener*, 1860, 82.
20. Deen, *Chronicles of a Minnesota Pioneer*, 7.
21. Share, Hortense, MSHS, *Annual Report*, 1877, 104.
22. Ibid., 104.
23. Yzermans, *The Mel and the Rose*, 19.
24. Jarchow, *The Earth Brought Forth*, 250.
25. *Minnesota Farmer and Gardener*, 1860, 83.
26. "Fruit Growers near Prairieville," *The Minnesota Monthly*, September 1869, 321.
27. Bost, 151.
28. Atwater, Emily, *Pioneer Life in Minneapolis*, 26.
29. Burris, 58.
30. Burris, 60.
31. Ibid.
32. *Minnesota Farmer and Gardener*, 1860, 187.
33. "Flowers, Sweet Flowers," 3.
34. Ford, "Autobiography," 281.
35. Groveland Garden and Nursery, *Catalogue*, n.p.
36. Ibid., n.p.
37. Ford, "Mrs. L.M. Ford," 40-42.
38. Ibid., 41.
39. Bishop, *Floral Home*, 153.
40. Ford, *Minnesota Farmer and Gardener*, November 1860, 32.
41. Ibid.
42. Ibid., December 1860, 49.
43. Ibid., May 1861, 147.
44. Ibid., 154.
45. Kreidberg, "The Up and Coming Editor," 200.
46. Ibid.
47. Ford, "Autobiography," 282.
48. "75th Anniversary of the Ladies Floral Club," 2.
49. Ibid.
50. Ibid., 6.
51. Ibid., 2.
52. Taafe, Florence, "Some Highlights in 62-Year History of State's Oldest Women's Club," .
53. Ibid.
54. "75th Anniversary," 5.
55. Ibid., 6.
56. Ibid.
57. Ibid., 7.
58. Enger, *A Century in Retrospect*, 6.
59. Alderman, *Development of Horticulture*, 6.
60. Ibid., 42.
61. Ibid.
62. Harris, John, "Flowers," MSHS, *Annual Report*, 1874, 87.
63. Van Ravenswaay, 10.
64. Tapping, "Who Was Henchen?," 2.
65. "August Schell Brewing Co. Pays Tribute to Founder," *New Ulm Review*, March 31, 1949, 1.
66. Van Cleve, Charlotte, "Bay Window Plants," MSHS, *Annual Report*. 1874, 44.
67. Downing, *A Treatise*, 63.
68. Tatum, "The Beautiful and the Picturesque," 42, 43.
69. Downing, *A Treatise*, 80, 81.
70. Tice, *Gardening in America*, 8.
71. Millett, *Lost Twin Cities*, 89.
72. Kennedy, *Architecture*, 478.
73. Ibid., 483.
74. Zellie, *LeDuc-Simmons*, 61-62.
75. Kennedy, 485.
76. Scott, *The Art of Beautifying*, 16.
77. Ibid., 14.
78. Ibid.
79. Smith, Cyrus L. "Landscape Gardening," MSHS, *Annual Report*. 1886, 230.
80. "Window-gardening," MSHS, *Annual Report*, 1876, 94.
81. Gregg, Mrs. O.C., "The Plant Window in Winter," *Minnesota Horticulturist*. 1898, 73.
82. Morris, *Old Rail Fence Corners*, 136.
83. Van Cleve, "Report of the Committee on Floriculture," MSHS, *Annual Report*. 1876, 36.
84. Wedge, Clarence, "Freeborn County Horticulture," in Curtiss-Wedge's *History of Freeborn County*, 241.
85. Tuttle, Reverend J.H., "Flowers," MSHS, *Annual Report*. 1876, 25.
86. Share, "Window Plants," 2.
87. Rea, "The O'Brien's House," 16.
88. Share, "My Flower Garden," 54.

89. Share, "Window Plants," 2.
90. Van Cleve, "Report of the Committee on Floriculture," 36.
91. Wedge, in Curtiss-Wedge, *History of Freeborn County*, 242.
92. Share, "Window Plants," 2.
93. Van Cleve, "Report of the Committee on Floriculture," 2.
94. Nagel, E., "Designing Flower Beds," MSHS, *Annual Report*. 1891, 254-255.
95. "The Elegant '80s in Minneapolis Society," 19.
96. Millet, 169.
97. "Full of Surprises," 788.
98. Van Cleve, "Old Time Flower Gardens," MSHS, *Trees, Fruits and Flowers*, 1899, 205.
99. "Mitchell Built House," *St. Cloud Daily Times*, n.p.
100. Baker, "Oakland Cemetery," 4.
101. Castle, *History of St. Paul*, 379.
102. Sloane, *The Last Great Necessity*, 44.
103. Farrell, *Inventing the American Way of Death*, 103.
104. Schuyler, "The Evolution," 295.
105. McKinnon, *A Green Hill Close By*, 3.
106. Farrell, 113.
107. Ibid., 121.
108. Baker, 4.
109. Kunz, *St. Paul: Saga of an American City*, 22.
110. Baker, 5.
111. Ibid., 11.
112. Tishler, "H.W.S. Cleveland," 281-291.
113. Baker, 14.
114. Olmsted County Historical Society, *Cemetery Inscriptions*, v.
115. Healy, George, "The Location, Laying Out, Planting and Care of Cemeteries," MSHS, *Annual Report*, 1878, 77.
116. Forest Hill, "Rules and Regulations," n.p.
117. Curtiss-Wedge, *History of Mower County*, 307.
118. "Woodlawn Cemetery," *Modern Cemetery*, 99
119. Atwater, *History of the City of Minneapolis*, 951.
120. Osteen, *Haven in the Heart*, 26-27.
121. Stone, "Modern Cemetery," 62.
122. Atwater, *History of the City*, 953.
123. Farrell, 117.
124. Osteen, 52.
125. "Floral Decorations," *Modern Cemetery*, 145.
126. Ibid.
127. Ibid.
128. Curtiss-Wedge, *History of Mower County*, 307.
129. Rudd, Willis N., "The Greenhouse," *Modern Cemetery*, 15.
130. Parker, J.G., "Greenhouses in Cemeteries," Association of American Cemetery Superintendents. Proceedings, 1895, 27.
131. Mendenhall, *Some Extracts*, 11.
132. Dolan, F.M., "Planting and Care of a New Park or Cemetery," *Minnesota Horticulturist*, 1903, 329.
133. Wirth, *Minneapolis Park System*, 17-18.
134. Castle, 370.
135. Curtiss-Wedge, *History of Winona County*, 842.
136. Andrews, 522.
137. "Immense Throng at Dedication of German Park," 1914. Clippings file "German park," at Brown County Historical Society. n.p.
138. Anderson, Torgny, ed., *The Cottonwood Community*. Cottonwood, Minn.: W.E. "Bor" Anderson, 1963, n.p.
139. Ubl, "New Ulm German Park History," n.p.
140. *A Brief History of the Irvine Park District*, 10.
141. Mitchell, *History of Stearns County*, 772.
142. Zumbrota Valley Historical Society, *Zumbrota*, 36.
143. Nussbaumer, Frederick, "An Ideal Public Park," *Minnesota Horticulturist*, 1902, 114.
144. Prantner, Development of a Park System, 10.
145. "Loring, Charles Morgridge," *Dictionary of American Biography*, vol. 6, 414.
146. Murphy, "St. Paul's Crystal Palace," 135.
147. Potter, "Como Conservatory," 13.
148. Peabody, "History of Parks," 610.
149. Ibid., 609.
150. Andrews, 524.
151. Peabody, 609.
152. Nussbaumer, "An Ideal Public Park," 114.
153. Monsour, "Vanished Park," n.p.
154. "Huge Granite Bullfrog ," 9.
155. Ibid.
156. "Caring for 82,000 Tender Plants One Task of 'Father of City Parks," no date or page; "Nussbaumer" clippings file of Como Conservatory, St. Paul.
157. Kelley, *City of St. Paul*, 14.
158. Ibid.
159. "Como Flower Show ," 7.
160. Ibid.
161. Ibid.
162. "Mayo Gardener," *Rochester Post Bulletin*, 5.
163. "Residence of F.B. Forman," *Western Architect*, 18.
164. Folsom, *More Great American Mansions*, 263.
165. Bernini, "Glensheen," 41.
166. Nutter, "'Highcroft,'" 16-17.
167. Waconia Heritage Association. *Waconia*, 85, 88, 92-93, 101.
168. Ibid., 92.
169. Terence D. Olson, interview, January, 1994.
170. *Mayowood, a Pictorial Guide*, 9.
171. Hellander, *The Wild Gardener*, 60.
172. Nelson, "Mayo's First," 36.
173. *Mayowood, Home of Dr. Charles H. Mayo*, n.p.
174. Olson interview, January 1994.
175. "60,000 Chrysanthemums," 9.
176. Ibid.
177. Ibid.
178. Olson interview.
179. Folsom, *More Mansions*, 266.
180. Chamberlain, "Glensheen " 8.
181. Senuta, "Glensheen Opens its Doors," 65.
182. Bernini, 33.
183. Senuta, 9 - 10.

184. Scott, *Duluth*, 5.
185. Chamberlain, 9.
186. Lane, "Glensheen—A Country Estate," 2, 3.
187. Dan McClelland, interviews with the author, November 1993 and January 1994.
188. Congdon, Chester, "Memorandum Book for Glenhome,"1910 [journal kept by Congdon], 65. Copies from Glensheen staff.
189. Copy of Clara Congdon's list of roses ordered from a Baltimore nursery in 1915, Glensheen.
190. Chamberlain, 8.
191. Fourie, *Their Roots Run Deep*, n.p.
192. Ibid., 2, 3.
193. Boutang, "Gardens of Glensheen," 38.
194. Ibid., 38-41.
195. Castle, 391.
196. Peterson, "The City Beautiful Movement," 415-416.
197. Red Wing, Minnesota, Planning Staff. *Levee Park*, n.p.
198. Garlin, Hamlin, *A Son of the Middle Border*, 458. Suggested by *Levee Park: Gateway to the City*.
199. Peterson, "The City Beautiful," 420.
200. Castle, 394.
201. Underwood, Anna B.,"A Season's Work with Children and Flowers," *Trees, Fruit, and Flowers*, 1906, 107.
202. Ibid.
203. "Anna B. Underwood," *Lake City Graphic Republican*, 2.
204. Underwood, "A Season's Work," 107.
205. Ibid., 111.
206. Underwood, Anna B., "A Third Season in Civic Improvement Work," *Trees, Fruit and Flowers*. 1908, 185.
207. Underwood, Anna B., "Fifth Year in Improvement Work," *Minnesota Horticulturist*, March 1910, 85.
208. Underwood, Anna B., "The Sixth Year in Civic Improvement," *Minnesota Horticulturist*, May 1911, 166.
209. Ibid., 164.
210. Red Wing, *Levee Park*, n.p.
211. "Civic League is Organized Here," 5.
212. Curtiss-Wedge, *The History of Goodhue County*, 512.
213. Ibid., 624.
214. "The Children Plant Trees," 3.
215. Curtiss-Wedge, 582.
216. "Improvement is Contagious," 5.
217. Hellander, *The Wild Gardener*, 153.
218. Ibid., 154.
219. Ibid.
220. Ibid., 68.
221. Ibid., 63.
222. Ibid., 155.
223. Ibid.
224. Mary Maguire Lerman, interview with the author, August 1994.
225. "Hitterdal Floral Park," 1.
226. Ibid.
227. Ibid.
228. "Local News in Brief," October 20, 1921, 10.
229. "He Builds English Gardens," *Fargo Forum*, July 4, 1937, n.p. Copy at Clay County Historical Society, Moorhead.
230. "Hitterdal—100 Years," 211. Information sheet from Clay County Historical Society.
231. "Local News in Brief," September 14, 1922, 8.
232. Philbrick, "Virginia Park System," n.p.
233. *Winona the Beautiful, Minneapolis, City of Parks and Homes, Minneapolis, the City of Lakes and Gardens* [1912 to 1915].
234. "Plan of Stillwater," 15.
235. Wirth, 166.
236. Ibid., 261.
237. Ibid., 29.
238. Ibid., 207.
239. North Central Florists Assn., 10,11.
240. Mary Maguire Lerman, interviews with author, July 1994 and March 1995.
241. Lerman, "Lyndale Park Rose Garden," 22.
242. Wirth, 209.
243. Lerman, "Lyndale Park Rose Garden," 22.
244. Wirth, 215.
245. Ibid.
246. "One of Minneapolis's Modern Factories," 11.
247. Lancaster, *Japanese Influence*, 223.
248. Lancaster, 223.
249. Lancaster, 206-207.
250. Great Northern Railroad President's file #542 B. Letter from T. J. Elliott to Mr. E. E. Nelson, July 24, 1929, 1.
251. Elliott's letter, 1.
252. Ibid.
253. Ibid., 3.
254. Ibid., 6.
255. St. Peter State Hospital. Minnesota Hospitals for the Insane. 10th Biennial report of the Board of Trustees. 31.
256. Oliver Iron Mining Company. Garden Report, 1921, n.p. In Oliver Iron Mining Company Papers, Minnesota Historical Society, hereafter referred to as MHS.
257. United States Steel pamphlet, 4. In Oliver Iron Mining Company Papers.
258. Lange, Dietrich,"School Gardens in St. Paul," *Minnesota Horticulturist*, April 1910, 121.
259. Ramsey County, St. Paul Board of Education. Division of School Gardens: annual reports, bulletins, and other materials, 1915, n.p.
260. Neeb, Edwin, "How I Raised My Garden," *Minnesota Horticulturist*, May, 1921, 135.
261. Netz, *History of the University of Minnesota College of Pharmacy*, 37.
262. "The Medicinal Plant Garden," 25.
263. Netz, 84.
264. *Minneapolis Journal*, May 17, 1936, Women's Section, 1.
265. Holmquist, *They Chose Minnesota*, 453, 366.
266. Dunn, Garden Book, 1903-1927. In James Taylor Dunn and Family Papers.
267. Richardson, Mrs. M.L. ,"Notes from Garden Clubs," *Minnesota Horticulturist*, 1940, 165.

268. *Moorhead Daily News*, September 9, 1930, n.p. In "Garden Club" clippings file from Clay County Historical Society.

269. Holm & Olson, *Home Landscapes* 1930, 3.

270. "Timely Garden Topics," *Minneapolis Journal*, May 29, 1938, 8.

271. Means, "Confessions of a Rock Gardener," 37.

272. *Moorhead Daily News*, August 18, 1936, n.p. In "Garden Club" clippings file from Clay County Historical Society.

273. Sanborn, "Minnesota's Largest Rock Garden," n.p.

274. "Alpha Chi Omega Builds Rock Garden," 5.

275. Lindgren, Ragna, interview with author, June 1994.

276. Ferndale Nursery, 9.

277. "Ak Sar Ben Garden to Close," 2, 3.

278. Ferndale Nursery, 10.

279. Benjamin, "Interesting St. Paul Women," 1.

280. "Extracts from Garden Club Reports," *Minnesota Horticulturist*, 1934, 112.

281. Ibid.

282. "Duluth Garden Flower Society," *Minnesota Horticulturist*, 1937, 16.

283. Ibid.

284. Minnesota Garden Flower Society Records, December 1,1935-November 30, 1936.

285. Minnesota Garden Flower Society Records. Clipping from *Minneapolis Tribune*, January 29, 1922.

286. Minnesota Garden Flower Society Records. Scrapbook.

287. Lake Minnetonka Garden Club, "Map and Guide for Garden Tour," 1946.

288. Richardson, "Notes," 105.

289. Gould, Mrs. E.W., "Garden Helps," *Minnesota Horticulturist*, 1935, 131.

290. Minnesota Garden Flower Society Records, scrapbook, clipping, "Oldest Garden Club in U.S. Notes 60 Years."

291. "Garden Clubs Report Birthday Planting Project," *Minnesota Horticulturist*, October/November 1985, 245.

292. Hodgson, R.E., "Bob Hodgson's Farm Talks," *Minnesota Horticulturist*, 1942, 79.

293. Minnesota Works Progress Administration, *WPA Accomplishments*, n.p.

294. *History of St. Cloud, Minnesota Parks*, author unknown, 18.

295. "St. Cloud Mourns," 4.

296. "Park Flowers are Damaged," 7.

297. Lehrke, "Park History," 5.

298. "Tulips Bow to Iris Rainbow," 11.

299. "St. Cloud Mourns," 4.

300. *St. Cloud Daily Times*, June 21, 1939, 8.

301. "Benevolence Blooms ," n.p.

302. "Greenhouse Crew," n.p.

303. "'Gates Ajar,'—Traditional State Fair Planting," *Minnesota Horticulturist*, v. 110, 1982, 200.

304. Marling, *Blue Ribbon*, 287.

305. State Fair greenhouse supervisor Rick Wimmer, interview with the author, June 1994.

306. Osterholt, "Two Noonan Parks."

307. Osterholt, 4, quoting an article by Luverne Heimer.

308. Ibid.

309. Osterholt, 4.

310. "Show Makes City Floral Center," 23.

311. "Opening Flower Show," 6.

312. Information from photos sent by the Virginia Area Historical Society.

313. "Giant 'Living Flag' to Bloom for Fair," *St. Paul Dispatch*, August 20, 1942, from State Fair Scrapbooks, MHS.

314. Gough, "Gardening for Victory, 22.

315. Ibid.

316. Much of the information on Victory gardens in Minnesota comes from two manuscript collections. The records for Duluth are at the Northeast Minnesota History Center. Records for Minneapolis are found in the papers of Frances Howe Satterlee at the Minnesota Historical Society. Both collections contain letters, news clippings, and brochures.

317. "Railroads Offer Land to Spur Victory Plots," *St. Paul Pioneer Press*, April 23, 1944. Clipping in Great Northern Railway Company Records.

318. Ueland, Brenda, "What Goes on Here," *Minneapolis Daily Times*, April 26, 1945.

319. O.S. Andresen of the Duluth Civilian Defense Council to Victory gardeners, May 14, 1943, Duluth Civilian Defense Council Records.

320. "To the Duluth Community Victory Gardeners," July 25, 1944, in Duluth Civilian Defense Council Records.

321. Satterlee to Minneapolis Mayor Marvin L. Kline, October 9, 1944, in Frances Howe Satterlee Papers.

322. Snyder, Leon C., "The Home Lawn," *Minnesota Horticulturist*, April 1953, 59.

323. Hard, Gustav, *Landscaping Your Home*. University of Minnesota Press, 1958, 3.

324. Clark, Clifford Edward J., *The American Family Home, 1800–1960*. Chapel Hill: The University of North Carolina Press, 1986, 211.

325. Ibid.

326. McGuire, *Gardens of America*, 9.

327. Hard, 3.

328. Ibid.

329. "Garden Editor Calls for More Dooryard Gardens," *Minnesota Horticulturist*, April 1950, 55.

330. Hard, "Dooryard Gardening," *Minnesota Horticulturist*, October, 1965, 103.

331. Williamson, *Lawns and Ground Covers*,7.

332. Ibid.

333. Stadherr, R.J., "Better Lawns—Through Research," *Minnesota Horticulturist*, April 1956, 36.

334. Ibid.

335. Ibid.

336. Northrup King collection at the Minnesota Historical Society.

337. Zakariasen, Russell Hamlin, "Yes 'Fine Art' Patio Design for Minnesotans, too," *Minnesota Horticulturist*, May 1960, 52.

338. Hard, C. Gustav, "Plants in Containers for the Patio," *Minnesota Horticulturist*, May 1965, 52.

339. Bachman, Ralph, "The National Rose Show," *Minnesota Horticulturist*, 1953, 12.

340. Dorothy Campbell interview with the author, July 1994.
341. Filson, Esther, "A Rosy Romance," *Minnesota Horticulturist*, June/July 1993, 16.
342. Hopper, Calvin, "Gladiolus Growing--How We Do It," *Minnesota Horticulturist*, May 1967, 58.
343. Ibid.
344. Boyd, "Urban Beauty," 8.
345. Price, Susan, "A Garden of Peace and Joy," *Minnesota Horticulturist*, August/September 1991, 7.
346. "B.H. Ridder Funeral Friday," 1.
347. Steigauf, "In Our Garden," May 11, 1952, 18.
348. Ridder, B. H., "In Our Garden," September 7, 1958, 4.
349. Ibid.
350. Blodgett,"A Man for All Seasons," 12.
351. Olin, "Edmund J. Phelps," 8.
352. Ibid., 9.
353. Ibid.
354. Ibid.
355. Blodgett, 12.
356. Friends of the Minneapolis Institute of Arts, *Green Trees*, 14.
357. Olin, interview with the author, May 1994.
358. Hard, "Minnesota Landscape Arboretum," *Minnesota Horticulturist*, March 1957, 28.
359. Karson, "Conversation with Kiley," 51.
360. Ibid., 50.
361. Eckbo, "Hideo Sasaki," 787.
362. Wilkes, "Hideo Sasaki," 344.
363. Lacy, *The Glory of Roses*, 19.
364. Ibid., 19-21.
365. "Veterans Memorial Rose Garden," n.p.
366. "Freeman Spade Starts Vet Memorial Rose Garden," 1.
367. Hazel Sweeney, interview with the author, July 1994.
368. Sheila Ubell, interview with the author.
369. Andraschko, "Winona Rose Gardens," 1.
370. Edstrom Frances Bowler, "A More Beautiful Place," *Winona Post and Shopper*, February 28, 1990, n.p.
371. *A Tribute to the Duluth Rose Garden*, n.p.
372. Ibid.
373. Helen Lind, interview with the author, June 1994.
374. Ford, Lyman, *St. Paul Daily Press*, November 10, 1876.
375. Snyder, "History of the Minnesota Landscape Arboretum."
376. Eisel, Mervin, "Minnesota's Number 1 Horticulturist," Information sheet provided by the Andersen Horticultural Library at the Arboretum Chanhassen.
377. "Founding Director of University Arboretum," 3
378. Olin, interview with the author, May 1994.
379. Olin, interview with the author, June 1994.
380. Olin, correspondence with the author, August 1994.
381. Ibid.
382. Eisel, "Minnesota's Number 1 Horticulturist," n.p.
383. McKinnon, Jane, "Leon C. Snyder 1908-1987," *Minnesota Horticulturist*, October 1987, 242.
384. Mackintosh, R.S., "American Association of Nurserymen," *Minnesota Horticulturist*, v. 58,:207 (1930), quoting University of Minnesota Professor Samuel D. Green at the 16th annual meeting of the American Association of Nurserymen in Minneapolis.
385. Price, Susan, "Mad about Glads," *Minnesota Horticulturist*, August/September 1992, 4.
386. "75 Years of Producing Hardy Fruits for the North," *Minnesota Horticulturist*, October/November 1983, 238-242.
387. Thompson,"Ye Old Time Minneapolis Gardens," 5.
388. Curtiss-Wedge, *The History of Freeborn County*, 238.
389. "The Father of Orchardists," 39.
390. Hutchins, A.E., "Historical Notes," *Minnesota Horticulturist*, June 1966, 73.
391. Ibid.
392. Ibid.
393. Qualey, "Diary of a Swedish Immigrant Horticulturist," 63.
394. Peterson, Andrew. Diary (Emma M. Ahlquist trans.).
395. Ibid.
396. Qualey, "Diary of a Swedish Immigrant Horticulturist," 68.
397. Ray, JoAnne, "Andrew Peterson, Early Society Leader Honored as Exemplary Emigrant to the New Land," *Minnesota Horticulturist*, October/November 1979, 242.
398. Alderman, 81.
399. Thuente, "Father Katzner's Contribution to Horticulture," 2, 3.
400. Katzner, Reverend John B.,"Experimental Work at Collegeville," *Minnesota Horticulturist*, December 1907, 441.
401. Katzner, "Collegeville Trial Station—at St. John's University," *Minnesota Horticulturist*, 1909, 45.
402. "Reverend John B. Katzner 1850-1930," *Minnesota Horticulturist*, 1930, 332.
403. "75 Years of Producing Hardy Fruits for the North," *Minnesota Horticulturist*, October/November 1983, 239.
404. Ibid., 240.
405. Barry, Neil, "Mums from Minnesota," *Minnesota Horticulturist*, May 1958, 51.
406. Eisel, Mervin, "Northern Lights Azaleas," *Minnesota Horticulturist*, March 1982, 68.
407. Olin, interview with the author, May, 1994.
408. Pellett, Harold, interview with the author, July 1994.
409. Alderman, 82.
410. "Nurserymen, Florists and Gardeners of Minnesota," MSHS, *Annual Report*, 1874, 10.
411. Brand, O.F., *Peerless*, 1895 Catalogue, Inside cover and 1.
412. Lake City [Minnesota] Centennial Publication Commission, *Lake City, Minnesota*, 30.
413. Wadekamper, Julius, "Minnesota's Royal Lilies," *Minnesota Horticulturist*, June/July 1982, 164.
414. Freeborn County Historical Society, *Freeborn County Heritage*, 562.
415. Boydstun, "Seeds of Enterprise," 110.
416. Lippincott, *Catalogue*, 1895.
417. Ibid.
418. Lippincott, *Catalogue*, 1899.
419. Boydstun, "Seeds of Enterprise," 108.
420. Northrup King, "One Hundred Years of Trust," 4.

421. Ibid., 28.
422. Ibid, 29.
423. Ibid.
424. Ibid.
425. Smith, Judge C.L. quoted in "Surviving Minnesota's Winter: Breeding Plants for Cold Hardiness," *Minnesota Horticulturist*, January 1975, 4.
426. Ibid., 5.
427. Olin, "Letter from England," 2.
428. Herb Baldwin, interview with the author, August 1994.
429. "Flowers, Sweet Flowers," 3
430. Fletcher, F.F. , "The Japanese Water Garden," *Minnesota Horticulturist*, 1911, 332.
431. Dr. Bardwell Smith, interview with the author, July 1994.
432. Smith interviews; Brown, "Contemplate Nature," 6.
433. "Jo Ryo En," n.p.
434. Smith interview.
435. Pat Barger, interview with the author.
436. Yvonne Bublitz, interview with the author.
437. Bublitz interview.
438. Here and below, Barger interview with the author; Bublitz interview with the author; "Normandale Japanese Garden," *Minnesota Horticulturist*, March 1971 and "Japanese Garden for Minnesota," *Minnesota Horticulturist*, August/September 1981.
439. Here and following paragraph, Barger interview with the author.
440. Bublitz interview with the author.
441. Ibid.
442. Here and following five paragraphs, Vera Trent, interview with the author.
443. Here and following three paragraphs, John Stoller, interview with the author.
444. Janice Bradshaw, telephone interview with the author, August 1994.
445. Ibid.
446. Query, Prudence, "Minnesota Monet," *Minnesota Horticulturist*, August/September 1994, 24-27.
447. Bradshaw interview.
448. Richard Beal, interview with the author, August 1994.
449. Ibid.
450. Bradshaw interview.
451. Beal interview.
452. Bradshaw interview.
453. Northrup King, *Sterling Seeds* (catalogue), 1915, 161.
454. Van Cleve, "Old Time Flower Gardens," 205.
455. Kennedy, Mrs. A.A., "Old Fashioned Perennial Flowers," MSHS, Annual Report, 1899, 344.
456. Van Cleve, "Old Time Flower Gardens," 205.
457. "The Hardy Garden," *The Minnesotan*, February 1916, 20.
458. "The Hardy Garden," 25.
459. Northrup King, *Sterling Seeds* (Catalogue), 1915, 161.
460. Bea Westerberg, interview with the author.
461. Ibid.
462. Larry Westerberg, interview with the author.
463. Bea Westerberg, interview.

464. Lou Hoppa, master gardener at the Heritage Garden, run by the Olmsted County Historical Society, telephone interview with the author, October 1993.
465. "A Visit to Time Past," *Minnesota Horticulturist*, June/July 1984, 171–72; interview with Mary Maguire Lerman, July 1994.
466. Here and below, Lerman interview, July 1994.
467. Marcia Qualset, telephone interview with the author, and information from the clippings file, Blue Earth County Historical Society.
468. Qualset interview.
469. Sandy Tanck, telephone interview with the author.
470. Here and below, Tim Kenney, telephone interview with the author.
471. Here and below, Bonnie Lawrence, interview with the author.
472. Pat Reed, telephone interviews with the author, February 1991, and July 1994; Duane Northagen telephone interview with the author, July 1994.
473. Reed interview, July 1994.
474. Reed interview, February 1991.
475. Reed interview, July 1994.
476. Ibid.
477. Northagen interview.
478. Snyder, *Native Plants*, 1.
479. Van Cleve, "Wild Flowers," MSHS, *Annual Report*, 1887, 307.
480. Bray, "Surveying the Seasons," 72.
481. Lange, "A Plea for Our Wild Flowers," *Minnesota Horticulturist*, 1912, 28.
482. "Make Minnesota Blossom," n.d., clipping, scrapbook, Minnesota Garden Flower Society Records.
483. Leonard, Jonathan N., "The Public and 'Silent Spring," *Minnesota Horticulturist*, April 1965, 44.
484. Here and following four paragraphs, Carol Kollander, interview with the author, August 1994.
485. Here and following three paragraphs, Charlotte Menzel, interview with the author, August 1994.
486. Here and following three paragraphs, Jim Hagstrom, interview with the author, August 1994.
487. Here and following four paragraphs, Dr. Charles Mason, interview with the author, July 1994.
488. Bobby Jensen, interview with the author.
489. Here and following paragraphs, Carroll Henderson, interview with the author, August 1994.
490. Here and following paragraphs, Nancy Gibson, interview with the author, August 1993.
491. Henderson interview, August 1994.

BIBLIOGRAPHY

Books

Abbott, Daisy T. *The Northern Garden Week by Week*. Minneapolis: University of Minnesota Press, 1938.

——. *The Indoor Garden*. Minneapolis: University of Minnesota Press, 1939.

Alderman, William H. *The Development of Horticulture on the Northern Great Plains*. St. Paul: Sponsored by the Great Plains Region American Society for Horticultural Science, 1962.

Andreas, Alfred T. *An Illustrated Historical Atlas of the State of Minnesota*. Chicago: A. T. Andreas, 1874.

Andrews, Gen. [Christopher] C., ed. *History of St. Paul, Minnesota, with Illustrations and Biographical Sketches of Some of its Prominent Men and Pioneers*. Syracuse: D. Mason and Co. 1890.

Atwater, Isaac. *History of the City of Minneapolis, Minnesota*. New York:Munsell and Co., 1893.

Atwater, Mrs. Isaac. *Pioneer Life in Minneapolis, from a Woman's Standpoint, 1840–1894*. Minneapolis: DeVeny Print Co. [1894].

Berg, Donald. *Country Patterns: A Sampler of American Country Home and Landscape Designs from Original 19th Century Sources*. Pittstown, N.J.: Main Street Press, 1986.

Bishop, Harriet E. *Floral Home, or First Years of Minnesota, Sketches, Later Settlements and Further Developments*. New York: Sheldon, Blakeman & Co., 1857.

Bost, Theodore. *A Frontier Family in Minnesota: Letters of Theodore and Sophie Bost, 1851–1920*. Minneapolis: University of Minnesota Press, 1981.

Brinkman, Marilyn S., and William T. Morgan. *Light from the Hearth: Central Minnesota Pioneers and Early Architecture*. St. Cloud: North Star Press, 1982.

Burris, Evadene Adele. *Frontier Homes and Home Management: A Study of Some Social and Economic Aspects of Minnesota Life in the Fifties, 1849–1861*. Ph.D. dissertation, University of Minnesota, 1933.

Castle, Henry A. *History of St. Paul and Vicinity*. 3 Volumes. Chicago: The Lewis Publishing Co., 1912.

Cleveland, [Horace] W. S. *A Few Hints on Landscape Gardening in the West*. Chicago: Janson McClurg and Co., 1871.

——. *Landscape Architecture, as Applied to the Wants of the West [and] the Relation of Engineering to Landscape Gardening*. Pittsburgh: University of Pittsburgh Press, 1965.

Curtiss–Wedge, Franklyn. *History of Dakota and Goodhue Counties, Minnesota*. Chicago: H.C. Cooper, Jr. and Co., 1910.

——. *History of Fillmore County, Minnesota*. Chicago: H. C. Cooper, Jr. and Co., 1912.

——. *History of Freeborn County, Minnesota*. Chicago: H. C. Cooper, Jr. and Co., 1911.

——. *History of Goodhue County, Minnesota*. Chicago: H. C. Cooper, Jr. and Co., 1901.

——. *History of McLeod County, Minnesota*. Chicago: H. C. Cooper, Jr. and Co., 1917.

——. *History of Mower County, Minnesota*. Chicago: H. C. Cooper, Jr. and Co., 1911.

——. *History of Renville County, Minnesota*. Chicago: H. C. Cooper, Jr. and Co., 1916.

——. *History of Wabasha County, Minnesota*. Chicago: H. C. Cooper, Jr. and Co., 1920.

——. *History of Winona County, Minnesota*. Chicago: H. C. Cooper, Jr. and Co., 1913.

Cutler, Phoebe. *The Public Landscape of the New Deal*. New Haven: Yale University Press, 1985.

Deen, Tilla. *Chronicles of a Minnesota Pioneer*. Minneapolis: Burgess Publishing Company, 1949.

Dick, Everett Newton. *Sod House Frontier*. Lincoln, Neb.: Johnson Publishing Company. 1954.

Dictionary of American Biography. New York: Charles Scribner's Sons, 1933. v. 6, 11 and 18.

Downing, Andrew Jackson. *Pleasure Grounds*. Tarrytown, New York: Sleepy Hollow Press, 1988.

——. *A Treatise on the Theory and Practice of Landscape Gardening*. New York: Funk and Wagnalls, a facsimile edition, 1859.

Drache, Hiram M. *The Challenge of the Prairie: The Life and Times of Red River Pioneers*. Fargo: North Dakota Institute for Regional Studies, 1970.

Enger, Lorna B. *A Century in Retrospect 1869–1969, The History of the Ladies Floral Club*. Austin, Minnesota [1969].

Farrell, James J. *Inventing the American Way of Death, 1830–1920*. Philadelphia: Temple University Press, 1980.

Favretti, Rudy J.; and Joy P. Favretti. *For Every House a Garden, A Guide to Reproducing Period Gardens*. Chester, Conn.: Pequot Press, 1977.

Fogle, David, Catherine Mahan, and Christopher Weeks. *Clues to American Gardening Styles*. Washington: Starhill Press, 1988.

Folsom, Merrill. *More Great American Mansions and Their Stories*. New York: Hastings House, 1967.

Freeborn County Historical and Genealogical Societies. *Freeborn County Heritage*. Albert Lea, Minn.[1988].

Griswold, Mac, and Eleanor Weller. *The Golden Age of American Gardens, Proud Owners, Private Estates, 1890–1940*. New York: Harry Abrams, Inc., 1988.

Guttersen, Alma A., and Regina Hilleboe Christensen. *Souvenir Norse–American Women, 1825–1925*. St. Paul: Lutheran Free Church Pub. Co., 1926.

Hard, C. Gustav. *Landscaping Your Home*. St. Paul: Agricultural Extension Service, University of Minnesota, c1964.

Hellander, Martha E. *The Wild Gardener, The Life and Selected Writings of Eloise Butler*. St. Cloud, Minn.: North Star Press of St. Cloud, Inc., 1992.

Henderson, Carrol L. *Landscaping for Wildlife*. St. Paul: Nongame Wildlife Program, Section of Wildlife, Minnesota Department of Natural Resources, 1987.

Holmquist, June Drenning, ed. *They Chose Minnesota: A Survey of the State's Ethnic Groups*. St. Paul: Minnesota Historical Society Press, 1981.

The Household Treasure, Containing Several Hundred Valuable Receipts. Philadelphia: Barclay and Co., 1867.

Jarchow, Merrill E. *The Earth Brought Forth: A History of Minnesota Agriculture to 1885*. St. Paul: Minnesota Historical Society, 1949.

Jeffrey, Julie Roy. *Frontier Women of the Trans–Mississippi West*. New York: Hill and Wang, 1979.

Jenkins, Virginia Scott. *The Lawn: A History of an American Obsession.* Washington, D.C.: Smithsonian Institution, 1994.

Kelley, Ann, and Philip Olson. *City of St. Paul, Como Park: A Romance, 1873–1973.* St. Paul, [1973].

Kennedy, Roger G. *Architecture: Men, Women and Money, 1600–1860.* New York: Random House, 1985.

Kunz, Virginia Brainard. *St. Paul: Saga of an American City.* Woodland Hills, Calif.: Windsor Publications, 1977.

Lacy, Allen. *The Glory of Roses.* New York: Stewart, Tabouri and Chang, 1990.

Lake City [Minnesota] Centennial Publication Commission. *Lake City, Minnesota.* Lake City, 1972.

Lancaster, Clay. *The Japanese Influence in America.* New York City: Walton H. Rawls, 1963.

Lanegran, David A., and Ernest R. Sandeen. *The Lake District of Minneapolis. A History of the Calhoun–Isles Community.* St. Paul: Living Historical Museum, 1978.

Langdon, Eustella. *Pioneer Gardens at Black Creek Pioneer Village.* Toronto: Holt, Rinehart & Winston, 1972.

Leighton, Ann. *American Gardens of the 19th Century; "For Comfort and Affluence."* Amherst: University of Massachusetts, 1987.

Marling, Karal Ann. *Blue Ribbon: A Social and Pictorial History of the Minnesota State Fair.* St. Paul: Minnesota Historical Society Press, 1990.

Mayowood, Home of Dr. Charles H. Mayo and Family and Dr. Charles W. Mayo and Family. Rochester, Minn.: Olmsted County Historical Society, [1965].

McGuire, Diane Kostial. *Gardens of America, Three Centuries of Design.* Charlottesville, N. C.: Thomasson–Grant, 1989.

McKinnon, Jane Price. *A Green Hill Close By (Mounds Grove Memorial Park, Evansville, Minnesota)* Alexandria, Minn.: Evansville Historical and Research Center and Douglass County Historical Society, 1986.

Mendenhall, Abby Grant Smith. *Some Extracts from the Personal Diary of Mrs. R. J. Mendenhall.* [Minneapolis, 1900].

Millett, Larry. *Lost Twin Cities.* St. Paul: Minnesota Historical Society Press, 1992.

Minneapolis Board of Education. *The School Home Garden Clubs, Garden Instructions, 1919.* Minneapolis, Minneapolis Public Schools, 1919.

Mitchell, William Bell. *History of Stearns County, Minnesota.* Chicago: H. C. Cooper, Jr. & Co., 1915.

Morris, Lucy L.W. *Old Rail Fence Corners: Frontier Tales Told by Minnesota Pioneers.* St. Paul: Minnesota Historical Society Press, 1976.

Netz, Charles V. *History of Minnesota College of Pharmacy, 1892–1970.* Minneapolis: University of Minnesota College of Pharmacy, 1971.

Olmsted County Historical Society. *Cemetery Inscriptions of Olmsted County Minnesota.* Rochester, Minn.: Olmsted County Historical Society, 1987, v. 5.

Osteen, Mame. *Haven in the Heart of the City, the History of Lakewood Cemetery.* Minneapolis: Lakewood Cemetery, 1992.

Parson, Ruben L. *Ever the Land, A Homestead Chronicle.* Staples, Minn.: Adventure Publishers, 1978.

Perkins, Alfred G. *School Gardening in St. Paul, Minnesota.* St. Paul: 1916.

Peterson, Fred W. *Western Minnesota Architecture, 1870–1900.* Morris: University of Minnesota at Morris, 1976.

Polasek, Emily M. K. *A Bohemian Girl in America.* [Florida] Rollins Press, Inc., 1982.

Prantner, Mary. *The Development of a Park System, Winona, Minnesota, 1890–1910.* St. Mary's College, 1993.

Punch, Walter T., ed. *Keeping Eden, A History of Gardening in America.* Boston: Little, Brown and Company, 1992.

Red Wing, Minnesota Planning Staff. *Levee Park: Gateway to the City Beautiful.* Red Wing: the Staff, 1979.

Rexford, Orcella. *101 Useful Weeds and Wildlings.* San Francisco: Denver, Hirschfield, 1942.

Scott, James Allen. *Duluth's Legacy.* Duluth: City of Duluth through the office of the Department of Research and Planning, 1974.

Scott, Frank J. *The Art of Beautifying Suburban Home Grounds of Small Extent.* Watkins Glen, N. Y.: American Life Foundation, 1977.

Sloane, David C. *The Last Great Necessity: Cemeteries in American History.* Baltimore: The Johns Hopkins University Press, 1991.

Slosson, Elvenia, comp. *Pioneer American Gardening.* New York: Coward–McCann, Inc., 1951.

Snyder, Leon C. *History of the Department of Horticultural Science and Landscape Architecture, 1849–1982.* St. Paul: University of Minnesota, [1983].

——. *Native Plants for Northern Gardens.* [Minnesota]: Andersen Horticultural Library, University of Minnesota Libraries, Minnesota Landscape Arboretum, 1991.

Soloth, Barbara. *Women on the Farming Frontier of Minnesota, 1849–1890.* Mankato: Mankato State College, 1965.

10th Biennial Report of the Board of Trustees and Officers of the Minnesota Hospitals for the Insane at St. Peter, Rochester, and Fergus Falls. St. Paul: Pioneer Press Company, 1898.

Tice, Patricia, M. *Gardening in America, 1830–1910.* Rochester, New York: The Strong Museum, 1984.

Van Ravenswaay, Charles. *A 19th–Century Garden.* New York: Universe Books, 1977.

Waconia Heritage Association. *Waconia, Paradise of the Northwest.* Waconia: The Heritage Association, 1986.

Whitney, Benson K. *Parks and Principles: Ideas in the Movement for Parks in Minneapolis.* Senior thesis, Vassar College, 1982. In the Minnesota Historical Society library.

Williamson, Joseph F. *Lawns and Ground Covers.* Menlo Park, Calif.: Lane Book Company, 1964.

Wirth, Theodore. *Minneapolis Park System, 1883–1944.* Minneapolis: Minneapolis Board & Park Commissioners, 1945.

Yzermans, Vincent A. *The Mel and the Rose.* Melrose, Minn.: Melrose Historical Society, 1972.

Zellie, Carol. *The LeDuc Simmons House, Hastings, Minnesota.* St. Paul: Minnesota Historical Society, 1989.

Zumbrota Historical Society. *Zumbrota—The First 100 Years, 1856–1956.* Zumbrota: Zumbrota Historical Society, 1956.

Periodicals, Pamphlets, Interviews

Aarstadt, Paul, Greenhouse supervisor Lakewood Cemetery, Minneapolis. Interview with the author, January 1994, at Lakewood Cemetery.

Abbott, Daisy T. "Growing Perennials." *St. Paul Pioneer Press.* June 10, 1932, Sect. 2, 1. "Our Minnesota Garden." *St. Paul Pioneer Press*, March 18, 1934, Sect. 2, 1.

Achter, Charles. "A History of the Progress and Growth of the St. Cloud Park and Recreation Department." n. p. Copy in Stearns County Historical Society, St. Cloud.

"Ak Sar Ben Gardens to Close in September." *Aitkin Independent Age*, August 29, 1979, 2–3.

"Alpha Chi Omega Builds Rock Garden." *Minneapolis Journal*, May 17, 1936, Women's Section, 5.

"Amateur Gardeners Prepare for Tonka." *Minneapolis Journal*, May 17, 1936, Women's Section, 5.

Andraschko, Bob. "Winona Rose Gardens." *Gazette Too*, May 17, 1983, 1.

"Anna B. Underwood Passed Away Saturday." *Lake City Graphic Republican*, November 20, 1929, 2.

Association of American Cemetery Superintendents. *Proceedings*. Chicago: Assoc. of American Cemetery Superintendents, 1888–1897, 1900, 1902, 1904, 1915, 1917, 1931.

August Schell Brewing Company ad. New Ulm, Minn. n.d. From clippings file of Brown County Historical Society, New Ulm.

"B.H. Ridder Funeral Friday." *St. Paul Pioneer Press*, May 6, 1975, 1.

Baker, Robert Orr. "Oakland Cemetery: 'A Safe and Permanent Resting Place.'" *Ramsey County History*, 16:3–22. St. Paul: Ramsey County Historical Society. 1980.

Barger, Pat, Ramblewood garden club member, Bloomington. Telephone interview with the author, August 1994.

Bassett, Thomas J. "Reaping on the Margins: A Century of Community Gardening in America." *Landscape*, Spring 1981, 1–8.

Beautiful Winona. Winona, Minn.: Joseph Leicht Press [ca 1900].

Beauty Grows with a Family, The Story of Bailey Nurseries Inc. and Its Founding Family. St. Paul: Dan Moriarty Assoc., 1989.

"Benevolence Blooms at the Virginia Clemens Rose Garden." Information sheet from the St. Cloud Parks Department in possession of the author.

Benjamin, Florence. "Interesting St. Paul Women." *St. Paul Pioneer Press*, March 18, 1934. Sect 2, 1.

Bernini, Nancy. "Glensheen in a New Light." *Lake Superior Port Cities*, January/February, 1982, 29–43.

Blodgett, Bonnie. "A Man for All Seasons." *Design Twin Cities*, Summer 1988, 8–12.

Board of Commissioners of the City of St. Paul. *Annual Report of the Board of Park Commissioners of the City of St. Paul*. 1895–1896, 1901–1902, 1904–1913 [St. Paul]: Globe Job Office, 1889–1914.

Boutang, Lisbeth. "Gardens of Glensheen." *Lake Superior Magazine*, April/May 1993, 36–39.

Boyd, Cindy. "Urban Beauty, Home Gardens Keep St. Paul Woman Occupied." *St. Paul Pioneer Press*, June 7, 1967, Sect C, 8.

Boydstun, Lisa Berkley. "Seeds of Enterprise." *Mpls/St.Paul*, March 1985, 108–110.

Brand, O.F. (Company), Faribault, Minnesota. "The Best, Peerless." Faribault: Brand, 1895.

——. *Faribault Nursery, Oldest and Best in Minnesota, 1858–1897*. Faribault, 1896.

Bray, Edmund C. "Surveying the Seasons on the Minnesota Prairies." *Minnesota History*, Summer 1982, 72.

A Brief History of Irvine Park District: The People and Architecture of an Extraordinary Neighborhood. [St. Paul, Minn.: n. p. 1986]

Brown, Seth. "Contemplate Nature, Inner Self in Zen Garden." *The Voice* (Carleton College Alumni Magazine), April 1991, 6.

Bublitz, Yvonne, Bloomington Greens garden club member. Telephone interview with the author, August, 1994.

Burke, S.L. and C.S. Wright. *St. Cloud, The Granite City Bids You Welcome*. St. Cloud: Greater St. Cloud Committee of the Chamber of Commerce and Federal Writers Project of the Works Progress Administration, 1936.

Campbell, Dorothy, St. Louis Park gardener and contributor to *American Rose Magazine*. Telephone interview with the author, July 1994.

Chamberlain, Carol. "Glensheen and the History of Garden Design." 1985. Sent by Glensheen staff. n.p.

"The Children Plant Trees." *Red Wing Daily Republican*, April 27, 1906, 3.

"Civic League." *Red Wing Daily Republican*, April 26, 1906, 4.

"Civic League is Organized Here." *Red Wing Daily Republican*, November 16, 1903, 5.

Clayton, Virgina Tuttle. "Reminiscence and Revival: The Old–Fashioned Garden, 1890–1910." *Magazine Antiques*, April 1990, 892–905.

"Como Flower Show Pleases." *St. Paul Pioneer Press*, November 8, 1915, 7.

Davis, LeRoy G. "Frontier Home Remedies and Sanitation." *Minnesota History*, December, 1938, 369–376.

Densmore, Frances. "Would Beautify City of Red Wing." *Red Wing Daily Republican*, October 31, 1903, 8.

Eckbo, Garrett. "Hideo Sasaki." *Contemporary Architects*. Chicago and London: St. James Press, 1987, 787.

Edstrom, Frances Bowler. "A More Beautiful Place." *Winona Post and Shopper*, February 28, 1990. From clippings file of Winona County Historical Society, Winona.

"The Elegant '80's in Minneapolis Society." *Hennepin County History*. Spring 1969, 19.

Eurich, F. "Landscape Gardening in Cemeteries." *The Modern Cemetery*. January 1892, 131.

Faribault Nursery Catalogue and Retail Price List. Faribault: Faribault Republican Print, 1871.

Farmer Seed Company Catalogue. Faribault: Spring, 1898.

"The Father of Orchardists." *Minnesota Calls*. August 1990, 39.

Ferndale Nursery. *Hardy Ferns, Wild and Garden Plants, Evergreens, Hardy Plants for Better Homes and Gardens*. Askov, Minn.: Ferndale Nursery, 1931, 1936.

"Floral Decorations." *The Modern Cemetery*. February 1892, 145; March 1892, 4.

"Flowers, Sweet Flowers." [St. Paul] *Daily Pioneer and Democrat*. Sunday, July 17, 1859, 3.

Ford, Lyman, M. "Autobiography." Minnesota State Horticultural Society. *Annual Report*, 1898, 282–283.

Ford, Lyman M. "Mrs. L.M. Ford and Her Flowers." Minnesota State Horticultural Society. *Annual Report*, 1897, 40–42.

Forest Hill [Duluth] Cemetery Board of Trustees, "Rules and Regulations of Forest Hill Cemetery." Duluth, 1927.

"Founding Director of University Arboretum, Leon Snyder, dies at 79." *News and Views*. September 1987, 3.

Fourie, Ada. *Their Roots Run Deep*. [Duluth, Minn.: 1985]

"Freeman Spade Starts Vet Memorial Rose Garden." *St. Paul Dispatch*, October 3, 1955. Sect. 2, 1.

Friends of the Institute [Minneapolis Institute of Arts]. *Green Trees, Halpin House and Gardens*. May 19–June 16,1979. Minneapolis: Friends of the Institute of Arts, 1979.

"Full of Surprises." *Hennepin County History*, Fall, 1961, 7–9.

"Garden Club." Photocopied news articles from the clippings file of Clay County Historical Society, Moorhead.

"Garden Lovers Offered Tour of Lake District." *Minneapolis Sunday Tribune*, June 11, 1933. Sect. 13, 1.

Giddens, Paul H. "Impressions of Minnesota Territory by a Pennsylvania Visitor of 1857." *Minnesota History*, Summer 1979, 211–227.

Gilman, Carolyn. "Perceptions of the Prairie: Cultural Contrasts on the Red River Trails." *Minnesota History*, Fall 1978, 112.

Gough, R.E. "Gardening For Victory." *Country Journal*, May/June 1993, 22–24.

"Greenhouse Crew Continues Fair's Floral Legacy." *Inside Infairmation*, April 1991, 1.

Groveland Garden and Nursery (Ramsey County, Minn.) *Catalogue of Fruit and Ornamental Trees, Shrubs, Roses and Dahlias*. St. Paul, 1855.

Haapoja, Margaret A. "She'll Even Promise You a Rose Garden." *The Senior Reporter*, May 1994, n.p.

Hagstrom, Jim, landscape architect in Lake Elmo. Interviews with the author, July and August, 1994.

Heimer, Luverne. "A History of Noonan Garden." Information sheet from the clippings file of Douglas County Historical Society, Alexandria.

Henderson, Carrol, Director of Non–Game Wildlife for the Minnesota Department of Natural Resources. Telephone interviews with the author, August 1993 and August 1994.

Hill, May Brawley. "Grandmother's Garden." *Magazine Antiques*, November 1992, 726–735.

History of St. Cloud, Minnesota Parks, ca. 1947, author unknown, 18–19. From the files of Stearns County Historical Society, St. Cloud.

"Hitterdal Floral Park." Information sheet from the Clay County Historical Society, Moorhead.

Holm and Olson. *Creating Your Own Landscape*. St. Paul: Holm and Olson, 1914–22.

——. *Home Landscapes*. St. Paul: Holm and Olson. 1913–14, 1920–21, 1930–32, 1934–36, 1938–50.

——. *Landscape Development*. St. Paul: Holm and Olson, 1911, 1920.

"How to Beautify Red Wing." *Red Wing Daily Republican*, December 16, 1903, 5.

"Hubbard House—Eternal Landscape of the Past." *Hubbardland*, Fall, 1977, n. p. From the clippings files of Blue Earth County Historical Society, Mankato.

"Hubbard Milling to Give Mankato a Park." *Mankato Free Press*, September 14, 1976? From the clippings files of Blue Earth County Historical Society, Mankato.

"Huge Granite Bullfrog Remains As Relic of Como Park Garden." *St. Paul Pioneer Press*, February 28, 1932, 9.

"Improvement Is Contagious." *Red Wing Daily Republican*, June 11, 1906, 5.

"J. P. Munsinger, Father of Park System, Is Dead." *St. Cloud Daily Times*, April 26, 1946, 1.

Jeffrey, Julie Roy. "There Is Some Splendid Scenery." *Great Plains Quarterly*, Spring 1988, 69–78.

Jensen, Bobby, landscape designer at Lyndale Garden Center in Minneapolis. Telephone interview with the author, June 1994.

Jo Ryo En: The Garden of Quiet Listening. Carleton College, Northfield, Minn. a brochure about the garden. n.d.

Johnson, Cora, garden club member in Nisswa, Minn. Telephone interview with the author, March 1994.

Jones, Harry W. "One of Minneapolis' Modern Factories." *Minneapolis Journal*, July 4, 1902, 11.

Karson, Robin. "Conversation With Kiley." *Landscape Architecture*, March/April 1986, 50–57.

Kenny, Tim, gardener at the Minnesota Landscape Arboretum in Chaska. Telephone interview with the author, July 1994.

Knowlton. "The New Building for Cream of Wheat." *Engineering Record, Building Record and the Sanitary Engineer*, October 27, 1904, 513–514.

Kreidberg, Marjorie. "The Up and Doing Editor of the *Minnesota Farmer and Gardener*." *Minnesota History*, Spring 1985, 191–201.

Lane, Michael. "Glensheen—A Country Estate." Information sheet sent by Glensheen staff.

——.*Glensheen, the Construction Years*. Duluth: University of Minnesota at Duluth, n.d.

Lawrence, Bonnie, community volunteer and gardener. Interview with the author, April 1993.

Lehrke, Mrs. George W. "Park History." *St. Cloud Daily Times*, July 19, 1945, 5.

Lerman, Mary Maguire. "Lyndale Park Rose Garden, 80 Years of Roses." *Minnesota Horticulturist*, June/July 1988, 10–11, 22.

——. Telephone interviews with the author, January and August 1994.

"Levee Park." Information sheet from Winona County Historical Society, Winona.

Lind, Helen, former head gardener, Duluth Parks. Telephone interview with the author, October 1993 and June 1994.

Lindgren, Ragna, St. Paul gardener. Telephone interview with the author, May 1994.

Lippincott, Carrie H. *Lippincott Flower Seeds*. Minneapolis, Minn: Lippincott Seed Co. catalogues from 1894 to 1910.

"The Local News in Brief." *Hitterdal Standard*, September 14, 1922, 8; October 20, 1921, 10.

Luxton, George. "Gardens Are More Vital Now Than Ever Before." *Minneapolis Sunday Tribune*, April 4, 1945, 4.

"Make City Beautiful." *Red Wing Daily Republican*, August 8, 1903, 8.

Martin, Frank E., and Thomas Oslund. "Minnesota Landscapes of the Modern Era." *Minnesota Common Ground*, Winter 1994, 1–2.

Mason, Dr. Charles, Director of the Linneas Arboretum in St. Peter. Telephone interviews with the author, November 1993, June and July 1994.

Mayowood—A Pictorial Guide. Rochester Minn.: Olmsted County Historical Society, 1988.

"Mayowood Gardener Goes to Europe for Specimens." *Rochester Post–Bulletin*, July 22, 1925, 5.

McClelland, Dan, horticulturist at Glensheen in Duluth. Telephone interviews with the author, September and November 1993, and February 1994.

Means, Joan. "Confessions of a Rock Gardener." *Horticulture*, April 1994, 34–37.

"Medicinal Plant Garden of the College of Pharmacy of the University of Minnesota." *Northwestern Druggist*, June 1911, 24, 25.

Menzel, Charlotte, gardener in Dellwood. Interviews with the author, August 1993 and 1994.

Minneapolis: The City of Lakes and Gardens. Minneapolis: Civic and Commerce Association, between 1912 and 1915.

Minnesota Farmer and Gardener. 1860–1862. St. Paul: Continued by Minnesota Farmer and Gardener and Educational Journal. 1862.

Minnesota Horticulturist, 1894–1994.

Minnesota Landscape Arboretum. "Major Developments Instrumental in the Growth of the Minnesota Landscape Arboretum." Available at the Minnesota Landscape Arboretum, Chanhassen.

——. "Chronological History of the Minnesota Landscape Arboretum." Available at the Minnesota Landscape Arboretum, Chanhassen.

Minnesota State Horticultural Society. *Annual Reports*. 1873–1898. Minneapolis: Minnesota State Horticultural Society.

Minnesota Works Progress Administration. *WPA Accomplishments, Minnesota, 1935–1939*. St. Paul: WPA, 1939.

"Mitchell Built House, But 'Grandmother' Made it Home." *St. Cloud Daily Times*, September 18, 1957. n. p. Clippings file of Stearns County Historical Society, St. Cloud.

Monsour, Theresa, "Como's First Oriental Park Vanished." *St. Paul Pioneer Press*, April 2, 1979. n. p. Copy in clippings file of Como Conservatory, St. Paul.

Moran, Dave, St. Cloud Parks Department. Telephone interview with the author, June 1994.

"Munsinger Gardens." Information sheet from the St. Cloud Parks Department, in possession of the author.

Murphy, Patricia A. and Gary Phelps. "St. Paul's Crystal Palace." *Mpls/St. Paul*, April 1984. Copy in clippings file of Como Conservatory, St. Paul.

Nelson, Clark W. "Mayo's First Agriculturist." *Mayo Alumnus*, Summer, 1987, n.p., copy sent by Olmsted County Historical Society, Rochester.

Nevins, Deborah. "The Triumph of Flora: Women and the American Landscape, 1890–1935." *Magazine Antiques*. 1985, 904–922.

Norcross, Marjorie R. "Cataloguing America's Cultural Roots." *Cornell Plantations*, v.47:15–22 (1992).

North Central Florists Assn., *Seventy–fifth Anniversary*. Diamond Jubilee held at Radisson North Hotel, Bloomington, Minn., 1983.

Northrup, King and Co. *Good Seeds, Northern Grown Tested*. [Minneapolis, 1897?]

——.*One Hundred Years of Trust, 1884–1984*. Minneapolis, 1984.

——.*Sterling Seeds*. Minneapolis, 1903–1919.

Nutter, F. H. "'Highcroft: Lake Minnetonka, Minn." *Western Architect,'* February 1903, 16–17.

"Oakwood Cemetery, Austin, Minnesota." *The Modern Cemetery*, January 1895, 127.

Olin, Peter. "Edmund J. Phelps: Gardens of Beauty and Balance." *Minnesota Common Ground*, Winter 1994, 9.

——. "Letter from England I." Arboretum News, September–October 1994, 2.

——. Director of the Minnesota Landscape Arboretum in Chanhassen. Interviews with the author, April and May 1994.

Olson, Terence D., Mayowood property manager. Telephone interview with the author, January 1994.

Olson, Jerry, Bloomington rose expert. Telephone interview with the author July 1994.

"One of Minneapolis' Modern Factories." *Minneapolis Journal*, July 4, 1903, 11.

"Opening Flower Show Gives City Real Summer Day." *Minneapolis Journal*, March 30, 1930, 1.

Osterholt, Minnie. "Two Noonan Gardens." 1990. Information sheets from Douglas County Historical Society, Alexandria

"Park Flowers are Damaged." *St. Cloud Daily Times and Daily Junior Press*, June 8, 1935, 7.

Peabody, Lloyd. "History of the Parks and Public Grounds of St. Paul." In *Minnesota Historical Society Collection*, v.15, May 1, 1915, St. Paul: MHS.

Pellett, Harold, coordinator of Center for Development of Hardy Landscape Plants at the Minnesota Landscape Arboretum in Chanhassen. Telephone interview with the author, July 1994.

Peterson, Jon A. "The City Beautiful Movement, Forgotten Origins and Lost Meanings." *Journal of Urban History*, August 1976, 415–434.

Philbrick, E. D. "Virginia Park System." *Epoch of Progress in Northern Minnesota*. 1915. Copy sent by Virginia Historical Society, Virginia

Phillips, Robert A. "Record Rose Convention Seen." *St. Paul Pioneer Press*, June 21, 1953. Sect. 2, 19.

——. "Test Garden Has a Rose Show." *St. Paul Pioneer Press*, June 18, 1961, Sect. 3, 5.

Pickett, Ida. "A Pioneer Family of the Middle Border." *Minnesota History*, September 1933, 303–315.

"Plan of Stillwater." Minneapolis: The Park Board, Morell & Nichols, Landscape Architects and Engineers, 1918.

Potter, Dean S. "Como Conservatory, The Jewel in the Crown." *Sun Country*, March/April, 1987, 13–15.

Prior, Jessie K. *Flower Seeds* [catalogue]. Minneapolis: Prior Seed Co., 1901–1902, 1906.

Purple Packages: Bachman's 100 Years. [Minnesota]: Bachman's, 1985.

Qualset, Marcia, gardener at the Hubbard House in Mankato. Telephone interview with the author, August 1994.

Qualey, Carlton C. "Diary of a Swedish Immigrant Horticulturist, 1855–1898." *Minnesota History*, Summer 1972, 63.

Ramsdell, Charles. "Architecture and Gardening in a Business District." *Western Architect*, 1907.

Rea, George A. "A Grandson Describes the O'Brien's House on George Street." *Ramsey County History*, Spring, 1979, 16–17.

"Residence of F. B. Forman." *Western Architect*, December 1903, 18.

Ridder, Bernard H. "In Our Garden: What We're Doing at 1033 Lincoln." *St. Paul Pioneer Press*, August 25, 1957, Sect. 3, 4; September 7, 1958, Sect. 3, 14.

Rudd, Willis N. "The Greenhouse in the Cemetery." *The Modern Cemetery*, April 1893, 15.

Russell, Maxine K., and Marion H. Trueblood. "Highlights of Fifty Year History of the Brainerd Garden Club." 1974. Typed article in possession of the author.

Russell, Maxine K., Brainerd Garden Club member. Telephone interview with the author, March 1994.

"St. Cloud Mourns Death of Father of Our Park System." *St. Cloud Daily Times*, April 27, 1946, 4.

Sanborn, Clint. "Minnesota's Largest Rock Garden, Arthur Johnsons Maintain Spot." *Minneapolis Tribune*, July 12, 1964.

Scherer, W.P. ("Walt.") "Cultivating A Garden In Southern Minnesota." *Mankato Free Press*, March 28, 1938.

——. "The Enthusiastic Gardener." *Mankato Free Press*, October 1, 1938; October 26, 1938; October 31, 1938.

——. "The Enthusiastic Gardener Says:" *Mankato Free Press*, January 2, 1940; January 13, 1940; May 13, 1942.

——. "Our Gardens." *Mankato Free Press*, September 15, 1956; December 17, 1959; December 23, 1959; May 15, 1962.

——. "Your Garden." *Mankato Free Press*, April 17, 1950; September 15, 1950; December 3, 1952; November 5, 1953. All articles by Scherer are copies sent by Blue Earth County Historical Society, Mankato.

Schmied, Emil. *Winona Beautiful: A City of Fair Proportions and Vigorous Life, a Suggestion of the Forces That Make It*. Winona: Leicht Press, 1909.

Schuyler, David. "The Evolution of the Anglo–American Rural Cemetery: Landscape Architecture as Social and Cultural History." *Journal of Garden History*, July–September 1984, 291–304.

Senuta, James. "Glensheen Opens its Doors to the Past." *Lake Superior Port Cities*, May/June, 1979, 6–13.

Share, Hortense. "Window Plants." *The Ladies Floral Cabinet*. New York: January 1874, 2.

——. "My Flower Garden." *The Ladies Floral Cabinet*. New York: April 1874, 54.

"Show Makes City Floral Center of World Nine Days." *Minneapolis Tribune*, March 28, 1930, 23.

Simonds, O.C. "Cemetery Gardening." *The Modern Cemetery*, May, 1893, 25–27.

"60,000 Chrysanthemums in Display at Mayowood Flower Show Which Opens Sunday." *Rochester Post–Bulletin*, October 31, 1924.

Sladky, Roberta, director of Como Park Conservatory. Telephone interview with the author, January 1994.

Smith, Bardwell, professor at Carlton College in Northfield and initiator of the
    Japanese garden there. Telephone interview with the author, July 1994.
Snyder, Leon C. "History of the Minnesota Landscape Arboretum (through 1975)."
    n.d. Copy available at the Andersen Horticultural Library in Chanhassen.
Stanke, Terry, volunteer at the Como Park Conservatory. Telephone interview
    with the author, February 1994.
Stoller, John, gardener and art dealer in Minneapolis. Interview with the author,
    July 1992.
Steigauf, Joe. "In Our Garden: What We Are Doing and How We Are Doing It!"
    St. Paul Sunday Pioneer Press, May 11, 1952, 18.
Stone, William. "What a Modern Cemetery Should Be." *Proceedings of the
    Association of American Cemetery Superintendents.* September 15, 1896,
    62–67.
Sweeney, Hazel, former editor of the Rose Society bulletin. Telephone interview
    with the author, July 1994.
Tanck, Sandy, coordinator of childrens' programs at the Minnesota Landscape
    Arboretum in Chanhassen. Telephone interview with the author, July 1994.
Tapping, Minnie Ellingson. "Who Was Henchen?" *Hennepin County History*,
    October 1942, 2.
Tatum, George B. "The Beautiful and the Picturesque." *American Quarterly*,
    Spring 1951, 36–51.
Thompson, Ruth. "Ye Old Time Minneapolis Gardens." *Hennepin County History*,
    April 1942, 5.
Thuente, Rev. Adelard. "Father Katzner's Contribution to Horticulture." Copy in
    the archives, St. John's University, Collegeville, Minn., 1938.
Tishler, William H., and Virginia S. Luckhardt. "H. W. S. Cleveland, Pioneer
    Landscape Architect to the Upper Midwest." *Minnesota History*, Fall, 1985,
    281–291.
*Trees, Fruits and Flowers of Minnesota, Embracing the Transactions of the Minnesota
    State Horticultural Society.* vol.xxvii, 1899–1920.
Trent, Vera, gardener in St. Paul. Interview with the author, July 1994.
Tribute to the Duluth Rose Society. Brochure from the Duluth Rose Garden, in
    possession of the author.
"Tulips Bow to Iris Rainbows." *St. Cloud Daily Times and Daily Journal Press*,
    June 4, 1937, 11.
Ubell, Shiela, gardener for the State Capitol Rose Garden. Telephone interview
    with the author, June 1994.
Ubl, Elroy. "New Ulm German Park History, New Ulm, Minnesota." Summary of
    Ubl's notes on German Park. February 10, 1994.
"Veterans' Memorial Rose Garden is Planned for Capitol Approach Area." *The
    Minnesota Legionnaire*, September 14, 1955, n.p.
The Virginia Story, Historical Souvenir Booklet of Virginia Centennial Celebration,
    July 14–17, 1949.
Wedge Nursery. *Catalogue*. Albert Lea, Minn.: Wedge Co., 1898.
Welcome to the Normandale Japanese Garden. Self–guided tour booklet.
    [Bloomington, Minn.] n.d.
Westerberg, Bea and Larry Westerberg, gardeners in Hastings. Interview with the
    author, September 1992.
White, Emma. *Choice Flower Seeds* [catalogue] Minneapolis: E.V. White,
    1900–1917.
Wilkes, Joseph H. "Hideo Sasaki." *Encyclopedia of Architecture, Design, Engineering,
    and Construction.* vol. 4: 144 (1989) New York: John Wiley and Sons.
Winona, the Beautiful. Winona, Minn.: Joseph Leicht Press, [1913].

"A Winter Pleasure." [St. Paul] *Pioneer and Democrat*, October 27, 1860, 1.
"Woodlawn Cemetery, Winona, Minnesota." *The Modern Cemetery*, June 1892,
    44–45.
Ziebarth, Marilyn. "On Gardening." *Minnesota History*, Summer 1992, 70–79.

Manuscripts and Archives
Agricultural Society, State Fair Scrapbooks, microfilm edition Minnesota State
    Archives, MHS.
Baird, Sarah Gates, Diaries and Account Books, 1870–1918, MHS Manuscript
    Collection.
Bullard, Polly Caroline. "Remembrance of Things Past: The Reminiscences and
    Diary of Polly Caroline Bullard" 1897–1911. MHS Manuscript Collection.
Capitol Area Architectural and Planning board. Veterans Memorial Rose Garden
    Records, 1955–1969. Minnesota State Archives, MHS.
Catherwood, Gertrude Sherwood. "Historical Sketch of Ladies Floral Club of
    Austin, 1869 to 1934." MHS Manuscript Collection.
Civilian Defense Division: Citizens Service Corps. Agency History Record.
    Minnesota State Archives, MHS.
Civilian Defense Division: Citizens Service Corps. Director's General
    Correspondence and Subject File. Minnesota State Archives, MHS.
Civilian Defense Division. Information Office Circulars and Bulletins,
    1942–[1945?].[A collection of circulars and bulletins, including information
    on Victory gardens.] Minnesota State Archives, MHS.
Duluth Civilian Defense Council. *Records, 1941–1946.* Contains clippings,
    correspondence, and leaflets about the Victory Gardening effort in Duluth.
    Northeast History Center, Duluth.
Great Northern Railway Company. *Company records* (1879–1973) President's
    Subject file 16404. Information on Victory Gardens. MHS Manuscript
    Collections.
Katzner, Father John, Papers. St. John's Abbey Archives, Collegeville, Minn.
Minnesota Garden Flower Society Records. MHS Manuscript Collection.
Northern Pacific Railway Company Records. President's Subject file 542. MHS
    Manuscript Collections.
Northrup King Company Records, MHS Manuscript Collection.
Nussbaumer, Frederick. Como Conservatory Archives, St. Paul.
Oliver Iron Mining Company Papers. Garden report, 1920, 1921. MHS
    Manuscript Collections.
Peterson, Andrew. Papers, 1854–1961. Diary, Emma M. Ahlquist, trans.,
    January 1, 1855–March 29, 1898. MHS Manuscript Collection.
Ramsey County. St. Paul Board of Education. Division of School Gardens: annual
    reports, bulletins, and other materials, 1915–1918. Minnesota State
    Archives, MHS.
Satterlee, Frances Howe Papers, MHS Manuscript Collection.
"Seventy–fifth Anniversary of the Ladies Floral Club of Austin, Minn. Oct. 1944."
    MHS Manuscript Collection.

INDEX

DESIGNED BY BARBARA J. ARNEY

TYPEFACE IS ITC GOUDY

PRINTED ON 100 LB. WARREN LUSTRO DULL

BY LITHO INC., ST. PAUL, MINNESOTA